PALESTINIAN WALKS

RAJA SHEHADEH is the author of the highly praised memoir, *Strangers in the House*, and the enormously acclaimed, *When the Bulbul Stopped Singing*, which was made into a stage play. He is a Palestinian lawyer and writer who lives in Ramallah. He is a founder of the pioneering, non-partisan human rights organisation, Al-Haq, an affiliate of the international Commission of Jurists, and the author of several books about international law, human rights and the Middle East.

PALESTINIAN WALKS

Notes on a Vanishing Landscape

RAJA SHEHADEH

P

PROFILE BOOKS

First published in Great Britain in 2007 by
PROFILE BOOKS LTD
3A Exmouth House
Pine Street
London EC1R 0JH
www.profilebooks.com

Copyright © Raja Shehadeh, 2007
Photographs by John Tordai

1 3 5 7 9 10 8 6 4 2

Typeset in Swift by MacGuru Ltd
info@macguru.org.uk
Printed and bound in Great Britain by
Clays, Bungay, Suffolk

The moral right of the author has been asserted.

A CIP catalogue record for this book is available from the
British Library.

ISBN 978 1 86197 804 2

The paper this book is printed on is certified by the © 1996 Forest
Stewardship Council A.C. (FSC). It is ancient-forest friendly. The
printer holds FSC chain of custody SGS-COC-2061

FSC
Mixed Sources
Product group from well-managed
forests and other controlled sources
Cert no. SGS-COC-2061
www.fsc.org
© 1996 Forest Stewardship Council

To my nephew and niece, Aziz and Tala, with the hope that they will be able to walk in the hills of Palestine.

CONTENTS

Palestine and Israel showing locations mentioned
in the text

○ Palestinian towns and villages inside the
West Bank and the Gaza Strip

● Jewish settlements inside
the West Bank

□ Other towns in Israel

*Lake Tiberias
(Sea of Galilee)*

Haifa

Tiberias

Nazareth

*Mediterranean
Sea*

Jenin

**West
Bank**

1967 Armistice line

Jordan

Nablus

Tel Aviv

Jaffa

Talmon Beth
Talmon

Al Janieh

Deir Ammar
Ras Karkar

Beit Eil

Lydda
Ramle

Beit 'Ur El Tahta

Dolev

Maaleh
Mikhmas

Deir Ibzi
Bet Horon
Beitunia

Ramallah

Jericho

Almon
Jerusalem

Mitzpe
Jericho

ISRAEL

Abu Dis

Kfar Adumim

Bethlehem
Maaleh Adumim

*Dead
Sea*

Gaza

**Gaza
Strip**

Hebron

Beersheba

0 ———— 50 kilometres
0 ———— 30 miles

PALESTINIAN WALKS

INTRODUCTION

When I began hill walking in Palestine a quarter of a century ago, I was not aware that I was travelling through a vanishing landscape. For centuries the central highland hills of Palestine, which slope on one side towards the sea and on the other towards the desert, had remained relatively unchanged. As I grew up in Ramallah, the land from my city to the northern city of Nablus might, with a small stretch of the imagination, have seemed familiar to a contemporary of Christ. Those hills were, I believe, one of the natural treasures of the world.

All my life I have lived in houses that overlook the Ramallah hills. I have related to them like my own private backyard, whether for walks, picnics or flower-picking expeditions. I have watched their changing colours during the day and over the seasons as well as during an unending sequence of wars. I have always loved hill walking, whether in Palestine, the Swiss Alps or the Highlands and outlying islands of Scotland, where it was a particular joy to ramble without fear of harassment and the distracting awareness of imminent political and physical disasters.

I began taking long walks in Palestine in the late 1970s. This was before many of the irreversible changes that blighted the land began to take place. The hills then were like one large nature reserve with all the unspoiled beauty and freedom unique to such areas. The six walks described in this book span a period of twenty-six years. Although each walk takes its own unique course they are also travels through time and space. It is a journey beginning in 1978 and ending in 2006, in which I write about the developments I have witnessed in the region and about the changes to my life and surroundings. I describe walking in the hills around Ramallah, in the wadis in the Jerusalem wilderness and through the gorgeous ravines by the Dead Sea.

Palestine has been one of the countries most visited by pilgrims and travellers over the ages. The accounts I have read do not describe a land familiar to me but rather a land of these travellers' imaginations. Palestine has been constantly re-invented, with devastating consequences to its original inhabitants. Whether it was the cartographers preparing maps or travellers describing the landscape in the extensive travel literature, what mattered was not the land and its inhabitants as they actually were but the confirmation of the viewer's or reader's religious or political beliefs. I can only hope that this book does not fall within this tradition.

Perhaps the curse of Palestine is its centrality to the West's historical and biblical imagination. The landscape is thus cut to match the grim events recorded there. Here is how Thackeray describes the hills I have so loved:

Parched mountains, with a grey bleak olive tree
trembling here and there; savage ravines and valleys
paved with tombstones – a landscape unspeakably
ghastly and desolate, meet the eye wherever you wander
round about the city. The place seems quite adapted to
the events which are recorded in the Hebrew histories.
It and they, as it seems to me, can never be regarded
without terror. Fear and blood, crime and punishment,
follow from page to page in frightful succession. There is
not a spot at which you look, but some violent deed has
been done there: some massacre has been committed,
some victim has been murdered, some idol has been
worshipped with bloody and dreadful rites.

(Notes of a Journey from Cornhill to Grand Cairo)

It is as though once the travellers took the arduous
trip to visit Palestine and did not find what they were
seeking, the land as it existed in their imagination, they
took a strong aversion to what they found. 'Palestine sits
in sackcloth and ashes,' Mark Twain writes. '... Palestine
is desolate and unlovely ... Palestine is no more of this
work-day world. It is sacred to poetry and tradition – it is
a dream-land' *(The Innocents Abroad)*.

The Western world's confrontation with Palestine is
perhaps the longest-running drama in history. This was
not my drama, although I suppose I am a bit player in
it. I like to think of my relationship to the land, where
I have always lived, as immediate and not experienced
through the veil of words written about it, often replete
with distortions.

And yet it is in the unavoidable context of such literature that I write my own account of the land and the
contemporary culture of 'fear and blood, crime and

punishment' that blot its beauty. Perhaps many will also read this book against the background of the grim images on their television screens. They might experience a dissonant moment as they read about the beautiful countryside in which the six walks in this book take place: could the land of perpetual strife and bloodshed have such peaceful, precious hills? Still, I hope the reader of this book will put all this aside and approach it with an open mind. I hope to persuade the reader how glorious the land of Palestine is, despite all the destruction that has been wrought over the past quarter of a century.

This long-running drama has not ended. The stage, however, has relocated to the hills of the West Bank, where Israeli planners place Jewish settlements on hilltops and plan them such that they can only see other settlements while strategically dominating the valleys in which most Palestinian villages are located. It is not unusual to find the names of Arab villages on road signs deleted with black paint by over-active settlers.

A sales brochure, for the ultra-Orthodox West Bank settlement of Emanuel, published in Brooklyn for member recruitment, evokes the picturesque: 'The city of Emanuel, situated 440 metres above sea level, has a magnificent view of the coastal plain and the Judean Mountains. The hilly landscape is dotted by green olive orchards and enjoys a pastoral calm.' Re-creating the picturesque scenes of a biblical landscape becomes a testimony to an ancient claim on the land.

Commenting on advertisements such as this, the Israeli architects Rafi Segal and Eyal Weizman percep-tively uncover 'a cruel paradox': 'the very thing that renders the landscape "biblical", its traditional inhabi-tation and cultivation in terraces, olive orchards, stone building and the presence of livestock, is produced by the Palestinians, whom the Jewish settlers came to replace. And yet the very people who cultivate the 'green olive orchards' and render the landscape biblical are themselves excluded from the panorama. The Palestinians are there to produce the scenery and then disappear.'[1]

The land deemed 'without a people' is thus made available to the Jewish citizens of Israel, who can no longer claim to be 'a people without a land'.

The Israel Exploration Society instructs its researchers to provide 'concrete documentation of the continuity of a historical thread that remained unbroken from the time of Joshua Bin Nun until the days of the conquerors of the Negev in our generation'. To achieve this, the intervening centuries and generations of the land's inhabitants have to be obliterated and denied. In the process history, mine and that of my people, is distorted and twisted.

Such an attitude fits perfectly into the long tradition of Western travellers and colonizers who simply would not see the land's Palestinian population. When they spared a glance it was to regard the Palestinians with prejudice and derision, as a distraction from the land of their imagination. So Thackeray describes an anonymous Arab village outside of Jerusalem thus: 'A village of beavers, or a colony of ants, make habitations not unlike those dismal huts piled together on the plain here ...' (*Notes of a Journey* ...).

I am both an author and a lawyer. From the early 1980s I have been writing about the legal aspects of the struggle

1 Rafi Segal and Eyal Weizman, 'The Mountain. Principles of Building in Heights', in *A Civilian Occupation. The Politics of Israeli Architecture*, eds. Rafi Segal and Eyal Weizman, Babel, Tel Aviv, and Verso, London and New York, 2003, p. 92.

over the land and appealing against Israeli orders expropriating Palestinian land for Jewish settlements. Here I write about one of these seminal cases. I also write about the disappointing outcome of the legal struggle to save the land for which I gave many years of my life. At the same time I explore the mystery of this divided place and my fear for its uncertain future.

Ever since I learned of the plans to transform our hills being prepared by successive Israeli governments, who supported the policy of establishing settlements in the Occupied Territories, I have felt like one who is told that he has contracted a terminal disease. Now when I walk in the hills I cannot but be conscious that the time when I will be able to do so is running out. Perhaps the malignancy that has afflicted the hills has heightened my experience of walking in them and discouraged me from ever taking them for granted.

In 1925 a Palestinian historian, Darweesh Mikdadi, took his students at a Jerusalem government high school on a walking trip through the rocky landscape of Palestine, all the way to the more lush plains and fertile valleys of Syria and Lebanon with their streams, rivers and caves. Along the way the group inspected the sites of the famous battles that were fought over the centuries in this part of the world, staying with the generous villagers who offered them hospitality. While the battles continue, it has been impossible since 1948 to repeat this journey.

During the 1980s, the Palestinian geographer Kamal Abdul Fattah would take his students at Birzeit University on geography trips throughout historic Palestine. One year I joined the students and we spent three exciting days travelling from the extreme fertile north of the land to its desert south, observing its topography and becoming familiar with its geological transformations and the relationship between geography, history and the way of life of its inhabitants. The trip was a great eye-opener for me. Since 1991 after restrictions were imposed on movement between the West Bank and Israel that journey too has become impossible.

The Gaza Strip has become completely out of bounds for Palestinians from the West Bank. A merchant from Ramallah finds it easier to travel to China to import cane garden chairs than to reach Gaza, a mere forty-minute drive away, where cane chairs, once a flourishing industry, now sit in dusty stacks. The settlement master plans published in the early eighties that I write about, which called for separate enclaves for the Palestinians, were being systematically implemented. To wrap up these inhuman schemes came the Separation Wall, which was not designed to follow the border between Israel and the West Bank but to encircle the 'settlement blocs' and annex them to Israel, in the process penetrating the lands of the Palestinians like daggers. As a consequence of all these developments even shorter school trips have now become restricted, so students can only repeat forlorn visits to the sites within their own checkpoint zone. The Palestinian enclaves are becoming more and more like ghettos. Many villagers can only pick the olives from their own trees with the protection of sympathetic Israelis and international solidarity groups. On Election Day in 2005 a young man selling sweets told me he was not going to vote. 'Why should I when I have not been able to leave Ramallah for five years now. How would these elections change that?' As our Palestinian world shrinks, that of the Israelis expands, with more settlements being built, destroying for ever the wadis and cliffs, flattening hills and transforming the precious land which many Palestinians will never know.

In the course of a mere three decades close to half a million Jewish people were settled within an area of only 5,900 square kilometres. The damage caused to the land by the infrastructural work necessary to sustain the life of such a large population, with enormous amounts of concrete poured to build entire cities in hills that had remained untouched for centuries, is not difficult to appreciate. I witnessed this complete transformation near where I grew up and I write about it here. Beautiful wadis, springs, cliffs and ancient ruins were destroyed, by those who claim a superior love of the land. By trying to record how the land felt and looked before this calamity I hope to preserve, at least in words, what has been lost for ever.

In Palestine every wadi, spring, hillock, escarpment and cliff has a name, usually with a particular meaning. Some of the names are Arabic, others Canaanite or Aramaic, evidence of how ancient the land is and how it has been continuously inhabited over many centuries. I grew up in total ignorance of any of these names. In this I was not unique. With hardly anyone now walking in the hills those with this sort of local knowledge are few and far between. With the help of the geographer Kamal Abdul Fattah and his students who interviewed old men and women who could still remember them, some of these long-forgotten names came to be resurrected.

Often, on my way home from a walk in the hills, twilight would descend and the stones along my path would be transformed in the half-light. I started seeing the shapes of figures in individual stones and would gather them up to take home. I picked up as many as I could, but once home I usually discarded them. The merciless light of my apartment bleached the magic from them, all except for one, which I have kept for a long time. The grey stone resembles a face with a large slit for a mouth open in a wail of horror. With what has afflicted these hills perhaps it was appropriate for me to have kept this one.

In the course of working on this book I came to realize that the writing itself was the seventh journey. I did not know where I was heading in this particular quest or how it would conclude. As the writing proceeded I realized that I was sometimes as guilty of omission and partial sight as those nineteenth-century travellers whom I had criticized. Throughout the book, the settlers, the main villains of my stories here, are a constant presence. I despise the aggressiveness of their intentions and behaviour towards my land and its inhabitants but I rarely confront them directly. They are simplified and lumped together, just as the nineteenth-century travellers generalized about the local 'Arabs' as they tried to obliterate them from the land they wished to portray. At various points the settlers are viewed from a distance. I fear what they might do. I wonder what they must be thinking. I ask whether I and my people are at all visible to them.

This last journey led to a confrontation with a young Jewish settler who had grown up and spent his twenty-five years of life in the very same hills. I knew that a large part of his world is based on lies. He must have been brought up on the fundamental untruth that his home was built on land that belonged exclusively to his people, even though it lay in the vicinity of Ramallah. He would not have been told that it was expropriated from those Palestinians living a few kilometres away. Yet, despite the myths that make up his world-view, how could I claim that my love of these hills cancels out his? And what would this recognition mean to both our future and that of our respective countries?

With the inevitable meeting that took place next to a settlement near Ramallah, my seventh journey, the writing of this book, came to its troubled conclusion.

1

THE PALE GOD OF THE HILLS

Ramallah to Harrasha

In the uneasy first years of the new millennium I felt that my days in Palestine were numbered. But whether Palestine or myself would slip away first was an open question. Cities were being erected in its midst, as were industrial and theme parks, and wide, many-laned highways more suited to the plains of the Mid-West of America than the undulating hills of Palestine. In two and a half decades one of the world's treasures, this biblical landscape that would have seemed familiar to a contemporary of Christ, was being changed, in some parts beyond recognition.

The biography of these hills is in many ways my own, the victories and failures of the struggle to save this land also mine. But the persistent pain at the failure of that struggle would in time be shared by Arabs, Jews and lovers of nature anywhere in the world. All would grieve, as I have, at the continuing destruction of an exquisitely beautiful place.

As a child I used to hear how my grandfather, Judge Saleem, liked nothing more than coming to Ramallah in the hot summer and going on a *sarha* with his cousin, Abu

1

Ameen, leaving behind the humid coastal city of Jaffa and the stultifying colonial administration which he served and whose politics he detested. It was mainly young men who went on these expeditions. They would take a few provisions and go to the open hills, disappear for the whole day, sometimes for weeks and months. They often didn't have a particular destination. To go on a *sarha* was to roam freely, at will, without restraint. The verb form of the word means to let the cattle out to pasture early in the morning, leaving them to wander and graze at liberty. The commonly used noun *sarha* is a colloquial corruption of the classical word. A man going on a *sarha* wanders aimlessly, not restricted by time and place, going where his spirit takes him to nourish his soul and rejuvenate himself. But not any excursion would qualify as a *sarha*. Going on a *sarha* implies letting go. It is a drug-free high, Palestinian-style.

This book is a series of six *sarhat* (the plural of *sarha*) through time and place that take place on various Palestinian hills, sometimes alone and sometimes in the company of different Palestinians from the past and present – my grandfather's cousin, the stonemason and farmer, and the human rights and political activists of more recent times, who were colleagues in my struggle against the destruction being wrought on the hills. There were other, less sympathetic, encounters that took away from my wanderings. Each *sarha* is in the form of a walk that I invite the reader to take with me. I hope, by describing what can be seen, heard and smelled in the hills, to allow the reader to enjoy the unique experience of a *sarha* in Palestine.

❧

There was a time, I'm told, when the hills around Ramallah were one large cultivated garden with a house by every spring. Olive trees dotted their slopes and grapevines draped the terrace walls. But by the late 1970s, when I returned from my law studies in London, these hills were no longer being cultivated. Except for the indomitable olive trees nothing that had been planted was growing in them. They had become an extensive nature reserve, with springs and little ponds where frogs hopped undisturbed and deer leapt up and down the terrace walls, where it was possible to walk unimpeded.

Ramallah was established some five hundred years ago by five clans. Its inhabitants depended for their livelihood mainly on the cultivation of the surrounding hills. My family belonged to one of these clans, but by the early years of the twentieth century they had left Ramallah, given up farming and joined the professional class in Jaffa, which they came to consider as their home. My grandfather Saleem served as a judge at the courts of the British Mandate over Palestine; my father practised law in the city from the office which he established in 1935. In 1948 they were both forced to leave the city of their choice. My father came to Ramallah, where I was born. My grandfather was exiled to Beirut, where he died two years later.

Unlike most of the other Ramallah families we did not own an olive grove, and during the olive-picking season we were one of the few who did not leave town for the hills, to spend the week on the laborious work of the harvest. If we ever ventured to the hills it was to picnic in springtime, when for a few months water flowed in the wadis. Otherwise the hills, so close to the house where we lived, were remote and foreign, little more than a derided buffer that separated us from the horizon where usurped Jaffa lay and at which we looked longingly in the evenings, when the faraway Mediterranean coast blazed with light.

My first encounter with the language of the hills was at the law courts, when as a young man I used to accompany my father, who was a recognized expert in land law. He took on many cases of disputes between landowners who possessed *kawasheen* (certificates of ownership) for unregistered land where the boundaries of the plot were described in terms of the physical features, in the language of hill farmers. It was there that I encountered such words as *sha'b, a'rsa, sabeel and bydar*. In later years, when the Israeli occupation forces became interested in claiming Palestinian land for Jewish settlements and I appealed against land acquisition orders to Israeli courts, the ambiguity in these documents was used against the farmers to dispute their ownership.

The land had a strong effect on the character of the inhabitants of Ramallah. The narrow slivers on the slopes of the hills were fertile but difficult to cultivate, and their owners had to depend on the unpredictable rains and springs. They were hardy, taciturn, closed-natured, suspicious and provincial. To go on a *sarha*, which was expansive, open-ended and uncontrolled, allowing the soul to roam freely, must have been liberating for the inhabitants of Ramallah confined as they were within the raggedy hills that offered no view of open territory or wide fertile fields.

In my family the practice was associated with my grandfather's cousin, Abu Ameen, who was already an old man when I was growing up. He had suffered a stroke and could only walk with the aid of a cane. I don't remember him ever speaking of the *sarha*; the stroke had made his tongue too heavy. My memory of him is of a short, silent old man shuffling around his dark, cavernous, musty-smelling home in the old part of town. It was from others that I heard about the *sarha* and Harrasha ('small forest'), where in the old days he used to spend the summer months cultivating his land and living out in the open fields, where Judge Saleem would visit him.

When I returned from my studies and began practising law in Ramallah, the occupation was in its eleventh year with little prospect of ending. Insidious but significant changes in the law provided strong indications of Israel's long-term policies towards the Occupied Territories, my home. Few seemed to be paying attention. A disquieting silence left me anxious and worried. Against the practices of the occupation both manifest and surreptitious and the restrictions traditional Palestinian society imposed on our life, the hills began to be my refuge. I walked in them for escape and rejuvenation.

In the beginning I did not know my way around. I would stray off the path, scrambling over terrace walls and causing their stones to tumble down behind me. It took a while before I began to have an eye for the ancient tracks that criss-crossed them and for the new, more precarious ones, like catwalks along the edge of the hills, made more recently by sheep and goats in search of food and water. Some of these were marked on Ordnance maps, others not. I found myself to be a good pathfinder even though I easily got lost in cities. As time passed I began to venture further and further into these hills and discovered new terrain, hills with different rock forma-tions, where flowers bloomed earlier because the ground was lower and closer to the sea.

The land around Ramallah is varied but without large open areas. It is part of the Central Highlands that dominate most of the centre of the West Bank. The valleys closer to town are narrow. The hills are steep, sometimes precipitous. There are no mountains anywhere in sight, only hills. The further west you walk, the lower and rounder the hills become as the land descends gently down to the coastal plain. All you can see are hills and more hills, like being in a choppy sea with high waves, the unbroken swells only becoming evident as the land descends westward. This landscape, we are told, was formed by the tremendous pressure exerted by tectonic forces pushing towards the east. It is as though the land has been scooped in a mighty hand and scrunched, the pressure eventually resulting in the great fault that created Jordan's rift valley, through which runs the River Jordan. The land seems never to have relaxed into plains and glens with easy-flowing rivers but has been constantly twisted and pressured to the point of cracking. Its surface is not unlike that of a gigantic walnut.

It was on the fertile plain of Marj Ibn A'mr (Jazreel Valley), which stretches below the Carmel mountains to Jenin in the West Bank and the breathtaking hills of Galilee, that most of the famous battles prior to the sixteenth century were fought and where the ruins of the fortifications and castles of the various invaders can still be seen. This was also the route of traders and pilgrims. No invaders or pilgrims passed through the hills of Ramallah however. The prize city of Jerusalem ten miles to the south could be reached from the narrow coastal plain through a valley that bypasses Ramallah by a few miles. The people in the village were protected by their hills. No heavy armament could be sent over the cracked terrain surrounding them. Nor was there much to entice conquerors. Only in 1901 was the first asphalted road opened between Ramallah and Jerusalem.

୬୯

It was on a spring day in 1978, the year of my return to Ramallah, that I stumbled, quite by accident, upon the legendary Harrasha of Abu Ameen, deep in the hills of Palestine.

It had been a long winter, continuing to rain throughout April and during the first few days of May, which is most unusual for this part of the world. I set out on my *sarha* just two days after the rain had stopped. The sun had emerged and the earth was not too muddy. The sky was blue with low scattered clouds that sometimes blocked the sun, making it very pleasant to walk.

My starting point on that day was behind the Anglican School in a north-western neighbourhood of Ramallah. I walked down the newly paved road, which continued northward towards the unfinished housing development, the farthest incursion so far of the town into the hills. I found the path almost immediately; once on it, a certain peace and tranquillity descended upon me. Now I could go on with no need to worry, just walk and enjoy the beauty of the nature around me.

I ambled alongside the western side of the valley across from the hill referred to as El Batah ('the duck'), so called because of the way it sits on the valley. Along the path the wild flowers were in abundance. Most were in miniature, blue iris only a few centimetres high, pink flax also very close to the ground and the slightly taller Maltese Cross and pyramid orchids, a colourful but thin carpet covering the vibrant land. I had assumed a pace that was neither hurried nor dawdling. I was heading towards the appropriately named Wadi El Wrda ('the flower') across the shoulder of the hill, a gentle descent that took me over one fold, down a small incline and up another in a diagonal trajectory towards the valley.

I could see that the wadi had longer grass and plants because it was fed by the sweet water of A'yn El Lwza ('the almond'). I crossed over and listened to the faint sound of the dripping of the water down to a pool. Then I bent and looked into the hollow in the rocks from which the water oozed. I stretched out my hand and let the cold water run over it. There were plenty of stones and weeds. The spring was in bad need of cleaning – otherwise the water would be gushing out. I sat nearby smelling the moist soil and looking at the impressive mossy brown cliff across the wadi. It was studded with cyclamens that grew out of every nook and cranny. They always seemed to grow in rocks that shied away from the glare of the midday sun, squeezing themselves between cracks to protect their bulbs from drying up. And despite their precarious position their delicate flowers grew straight up and were hooked at the top like a shepherd's staff. Their large round variegated leaves, similar to those of the grapevines but thicker, rounder and with a deeper green, seemed suspended from nowhere, miraculously hanging on the high steep rock as though trickling down it. The pink and red flowers were like randomly placed candles on an enormous Christmas tree. Above the cliff the hill was steep and from this vantage point seemed high and formidable.

Nearby I found a well-preserved *qasr*. The word, which literally means a 'castle', refers to the mainly round stone structures dotting the land where farmers kept their produce and slept on the open roof. It was in one of these structures that my grandfather, Saleem and Abu Ameen camped out when they went on their *sarha* together. It must have taken a good degree of skill to build one on this slope, where it has lasted for over a hundred years. Nearby was an old cistern. Before visiting the *qasr*, I took a moment to look around. It was as though the earth was exploding with beauty and colour and had thrown from its bosom wonderful gifts without any human intervention. I wanted to cry out in celebration of this splendour. As I shouted 'S-A-R-H-A' I felt I was breaking the silence of the past, a silence that had enveloped this place for a long time. My cry of greeting echoed against one hill then another and another, returning to me fainter and fainter until I felt I had somehow touched the entire landscape that surrounded this architectural wonder.

Along the terrace wall was a rock rose bush with its thick leaves and muted pink flowers. It climbed hesitantly over the stones, green against the grey as if someone had carefully chosen it to decorate this ancient wall. The stones with which the wall was built were carefully picked and piled together, and had held back the soil over many years without a single one of them falling, come rain or flood. Between these neatly arranged rocks more cyclamens grew. Their flowers stood at a thirty-degree angle like pink and red droppings all across the wall. In an opening in the stone wall between the two terraces were three wide stone steps placed there to make it easier to move between the two gardens. By the side of the steps was a yellow broom with its spiky green leaves. Its sweet smell filled the air. Lower down were some tall white asphodels and lower still bunches of blue sage. Even the long grass that grew along some parts of the wall added colour and texture. And when I looked up at the next level, I saw another beautiful garden, graced by a fabulous olive tree many centuries old, whose shallow roots were like thick arteries clinging together, clasping the ground firmly, forming a perfect wooden furrowed seat on which to sit and rest one's back against the trunk. Above this garden there was another. This terrace was large enough for two olive trees surrounded by a carpet of colour that spread all the way to the wall that led to yet another garden above, one garden hanging on top of another and another, going up as far up as the eye could see. I felt I could sit all day next to this *qasr* and feast my eyes on this wonderful creation. What fortunate people once lived in this veritable paradise. And how wide of the mark was Herman Melville, who described this area as barren when he visited it in the middle of the nineteenth century:

> Whitish mildew pervading whole tracts of landscape – bleached-leprosy-encrustations of curses-old cheese-bones of rocks, – crunched, knawed, and mumbled – mere refuse and rubbish of creation – like that laying outside of Jaffa Gate – all Judea seems to have been accumulations of this rubbish.
>
> *(Journals of a Visit to Europe and the Levant: October 11, 1856–May 6, 1857)*

I did not want to dwell on the vilification by Western travellers of this precious land and instead turned my mind to Abu Ameen, wondering how he managed his summers here. Was life in one of these *qasrs* so difficult that he never had time to stop and look at these gorgeous surroundings as I was doing? Perhaps he didn't need to stop to look. Perhaps his entire time in the hills with Saleem was one long *sarha* such as I might never be able to achieve.

The ponds along the wadi were filled with water from the spring. They had plenty of frogs, high spearmint, the common reed, and swathes of algae floating in the water, an unusual sight in these dry hills. This section of the wadi, called Wadi Qasrya, was wider, with the low hills on both sides seeming to recline further and further back. Coming down their sides were several small wadis, Wadi Shomr ('fennel') and Wadi El A'rsh ('the throne'). I left Wadi Qasrya and began climbing the high hill to the north with the ruin of Khirbet Sakrya, of which only a few stone houses have remained.

As I walked up I looked at the unterraced hill to my left. What would it take to clear this and terrace it, I wondered. What a feat it must have been to look at the wild hill and plan the subdivisions. How did they know when to build the terrace wall in a straight line, when in a curve and when to be satisfied with a round enclave where only a single tree could be planted? They must have been very careful to follow the natural contours, memorizing the whole slope before deciding how to subdivide it. The large rocks that could not be moved were kept standing where they found them. Here and there one could see clusters of them. Where they could, they made a small bay between them, an enclave, like a dimple in the face of the hill where a single tree could be planted. The terracing snaked down the slope to the wadi on one side and trailed up on the other, curving with the folds of the hill, always leaving a passage for the mule-drawn hand-plough to pass. Where once was a steep hill there was now a series of gradually descending terraces. In this way my ancestors reclaimed the wild, possessed and domesticated it, making it their own.

I was about to continue with my walk when I heard a rustle. I was afraid it would be a pack of wild dogs. With trepidation I looked up and saw instead a group of seven grey gazelles the colour of the rocks, running up the hill, taking big strides with their long thin legs, jumping so effortlessly over the large boulders that no stones tumbled in their wake.

I continued my slow ascent, following the silent musings of my mind and smelling the sharp brittle scent of thyme, which was growing in abundance on the side of the hill. My peace was shattered, when, out of nowhere, a huge grey bird flew right at me, its wings spread wide. I fell to the ground. It was an owl with a wingspread of a metre. It flew across to the opposite hill and landed on a rock, waiting to see whether I would pass and leave its nest in peace. On the side of the hill where it perched I could discern another *qasr*, which was built entirely in the rocks. The bird seemed to be indicating that if I attacked its young, it would know what to do with me and so I moved away quickly.

When I got around the high hill, a new vista opened up. The hills south of the village of Abu Qash spread out like the high waves of a turbulent sea all the way to the west. I now had to cross Wadi Matar ('rain'), along which ran an excellent path leading to the village. I managed to negotiate my way between the thickets. A smell of oregano from low bushes on the path lingered where I brushed against them. I had seen another imposing round *qasr* and was heading towards it.

The path took me behind the *qasr*, where I saw a cistern that the owners must have dug. I walked by the rusty metal cover in the ground and then over the fields, which had been cleared of stones. A copse of pines was growing there, the branches rustling in the light wind. I circled round to the front. As I stood before the door I had a sense of the family who must once have lived here. But no one was home, all was abandoned; except, perhaps, for the spirits. On this walk I had passed at least a dozen abandoned *qasrs*. Those who had once inhabited them were gone, that way of life was no more. Their owners had moved on to other places. At a certain point the land ceased to be capable of sustaining those cultivating it and other more lucrative opportunities for making a living opened up in the petroleum-rich Gulf and the New World. When I met Fareed, who originally came from Ramallah, at his palatial house in the suburbs of Washington, DC, he told me how, when he was a child growing up in Ramallah in the late thirties, his family could not afford to buy him shoes. So he had to make do year after year with his old shoes, which his feet had outgrown. His strongest memory of growing up in Ramallah was of pressed toes cramped in tight shoes.

Under Israeli law, Fareed and those members of my family who were not residing in the West Bank when Israel occupied it in June 1967 and carried out that first crucial census are considered absentees and their property outside the town has been taken from them. It was vested in the Israeli state for the exclusive use of Israeli Jews. I had read the law making this possible many times but its full import never struck me as it did now. A Palestinian only has the right to the property he resides in. Once he leaves it for whatever reason it ceases to be his, it 'reverts back' to those whom the Israeli system considers the original, rightful owners of 'Judea and Samaria',

the Jewish people, wherever they might be. Abandonment, which began as an economic imperative in some
instances and a choice in others, had acquired legal and
political implications with terrifying consequences.

When I had rested I threw a stone through the small
door into the dark interior of the *qasr*, not to drive out
the ghosts, which I don't believe in, but to scare off any
animals or creepy-crawlies that might be lurking there.
Then I entered, bowing my head. Inside, the air was
heavy, humid with a hint of animal dung. There was just
enough light filtering through the cracks between the
stones to make out the spiral stairs that hugged the inside
of the round structure and led to the second level. With
my hands extended in front of me to feel my way in the
semi-darkness I climbed up, keeping my head down for
the roof was low. When I emerged I found myself on the
first floor, where there were three deep-set windows with
wide sills. Here it was not as dark as the ground floor;
the air was lighter and fresher. Light came through the
low windows and bounced off the wet stones on the side.
But I did not want to linger. There was another staircase
leading up to the roof. I took it and emerged from a low,
covered landing on to the top of the unusually high two-
floor *qasr*. The roof was surrounded by a half-metre-high
wall with embrasures. It was not paved but covered with
earth and pebbles out of which grew small weeds.

I didn't stay long on the roof either. The sun was high
and strong. I made my way down and when I got to the
first floor found the shady coolness welcoming. I curled
myself over the windowsill and rested.

Through my window I looked at the fields across the
valley. The ground was carefully terraced in an almost
perfect crescent, the olive trees were evenly spaced

and the field between them was cleared of stones. The surrounding area was wild and chaotic, the terracing was half completed and many of the fields were covered with wild shrubs and thickets. I wondered who the owner of this *qasr* was and marvelled at his industry. I could imagine him sitting by this window, as I was doing, and surveying his possessions. Perhaps he had a number of children whom he observed from this watchtower and hurled orders at: 'You, Muneer, pick up those stones over there and plough the land around that plum tree.' 'You, Fareed, water that aubergine plant over there.' With water from the cistern they could plant all sorts of vegetables in addition to the fruit trees. And then when they harvested the fruit of their labours they must have walked or taken the mule eastward into Abu Kash and from there on to Ramallah. They might have followed the same path I took. With a heavily loaded mule it must have taken them much longer.

It was as though in this *qasr* time was petrified into an eternal present, making it possible for me to reconnect with my dead ancestor through this architectural wonder. Would this turn into the *sarha* I had long yearned to take? I was hoping, waiting, when my eyes fell on a large boulder that lay not far from the door. I wanted to examine it more closely, so I walked down the dark spiral stairs to the ground floor, bent my head and left as I had come in, through the small door to the field outside. Once my eyes adjusted to the glare I took a closer look at this large, oddly placed rock.

It appeared to emerge from the ground but did not seem to belong there. It rested at a strange angle. What was it doing here? All around it the ground had been cleared of large rocks. Was this one too big to remove and so had been let be? Or had someone brought it here? But why? What use could there be for a rock of this size in the middle of what must have been the garden? I began to circle it, examining it carefully. It was covered with soil. I began to scrape at it. The more dirt I removed the more of it I found. This made me more curious. What would I find buried beneath it? The deeper I dug the harder it was because the soil was more tightly packed. I couldn't scrape any more using my bare hands. I went looking for a sharp rock to use as a chisel. I found one and returned to the rock. The soil was so hard I had to use another rock to drive the chisel down. This way I was able to carve out a large chunk of earth, which broke off, bringing down with it a big section and revealing this stone was not in fact a rectangular block. What powerful forces of nature had hollowed this stone out?

Now that I had found this point of weakness the work became easier. It was clear that the rear of the rock was higher than the two parallel sides, which were of the same height. This could not be the haphazard work of nature. Someone had worked on this rock. I laboured faster now, not heeding where the soil was being scattered. I was getting more of it on my face. I could feel and taste it on my lips. Without stopping I blew to get it away. A finer layer of soil flew out of the sides of the stone, revealing clear marks of a metal chisel. This then was the work of a sculptor. But what was it? What was he trying to create? The stone on the back had sharp angles but on the side they were soft and curved. They looked like two arms. Or were they paws? Could this be a pharaonic statue of a sphinx? My heart was beating fast. I felt I was at the moment of a great discovery. The soil I was scraping more vigorously than ever now was blowing all over my face and clothes. My thick eyebrows and hair were covered with a fine layer of silt, turning me into some sort of maniacal living sculpture. In a brief time I had dug soil out to a depth of some fifty centimetres, reaching down to the flat bottom of this rock. When I passed my hand over it and swept off the last bits of soil I realized that I had cleared away the hollow of a carved high seat.

I turned around and sat down. Immediately I found myself settling into a precisely proportioned chair. The depth and angle were just right, giving excellent support to my back. The height was also right, allowing my short legs to rest flatly on the ground, relieving the pressure from my spine. And my two elbows fitted comfortably in the dips of the armrests, which were of the perfect height for my arms. Whoever had designed this must have had similar proportions to mine. I settled myself in this monumental seat and did not want to move.

A gentle breeze blew in my dusty face. My entire body relaxed from my neck down to my feet, and I settled more deeply in the stone seat and felt a perfect sense of peace come upon me. The view from the seat was not obscured by the *qasr*; it took in the full view of the fields which I assumed belonged to the owner of this summer mansion, who had not only this *qasr* but also his own *a'rsh* ('throne'). And then I remembered hearing as a child that Abu Ameen, my grandfather's cousin, had in Harrasha an *a'rsh* next to his *qasr*. Could this be it? Could this be Harrasha where Abu Ameen and my grandfather Saleem used to go for their *sarha*?

As I sat there on the *a'rsh* the whispers of the pine trees sounded like the conversation of a family gathered in a circle in their garden. As I listened the memories of

Abu Ameen and the kind of life he lived began to come back.

He was a quiet old man with grey hair and a cane whose hooked end was like the pale curve of the bald crown of his head and as smooth, not unlike the bent tip of the stalk of a cyclamen. As a child I continued to marvel at the incongruity of a man of modest means like Abu Ameen owning a *qasr* and having an *a'rsh*, until I realized that the *qasr* shared nothing with a castle except the ostentatious name. One day someone pointed out the collapsed stone structure next to our house and said it was a *qasr*. After this it was only the *a'rsh* that I continued to wonder about.

The half-demolished *qasr* in the field next to our house must have been built when the area was still uninhabited, because these structures served a purpose only in places far away from built-up areas. My childhood friend, Issa Mitri, and I used to play on the top of this collapsed building. We would pretend that a djinn lived under the stones and that if we turned them over he would escape. We never dared try to enter the *qasr*. When I heard how Abu Ameen used to travel to the hills and live in a *qasr* for six months of the year, I was filled with admiration. It was difficult to imagine the Abu Ameen I knew could be the same man as the adventurer who spent half the year in the wild, going on a *sarha*, and living alone in Harrasha.

Abu Ameen, whose first name was Ayoub, was my mother's second uncle from her father's side. The two men were very different. As children they both went to the same school established by English missionaries. Unlike his cousin, Ayoub did not like school. He found it too confining. It did not give him the kind of knowledge he thought was practical and useful. Saleem was the bright student who contradicted the teacher and seemed to know more than him. Abu Ameen found his cousin annoying and disruptive. He never understood why he bothered with studies and took his education so seriously. His strategy was to just let the day pass, and then the year, and then they'd be off and out of this prison called school.

Neither of them owned any land; they came from modest families. But he, Ayoub, was determined to acquire some. After leaving school he planned to work as a stonemason. There was much to be done. He would work hard and save money, enough to buy him a plot as close as possible to Ramallah. Then, after he had cleared it, he would use his masonry skills to build a *qasr* there, one of the best in the hills. He would marry, have children and his happiness would be complete. Saleem, who had entirely different aspirations for himself, was appalled when Ayoub told him of his plans.

'What?' he asked his cousin, incredulous. 'A stonemason? Is this all you aspire to make of yourself?'

'And what's wrong with that?'

'But don't you want to go to university? Don't you want to better yourself?'

'I'm happy the way I am. There is enough work for a stonemason; I will never be short of work. And you think it is easy work? It is very complicated and not anyone can do it. I am confident of myself. I will start as soon as this school year ends.'

'So this is why you have not been studying for the Oxbridge entrance examinations.'

'What use are these exams? You think if I succeeded I would find someone to support me through university?'

'This is no excuse. You can work your way as I'm planning to do.'

'Work for others when I have enough work to do for myself? Am I mad? You can go wherever you want. I'm staying here, in Ramallah. I'm not going to budge whatever happens.'

Saleem followed through with his plans, went to the United States and studied law. He did not return to Ramallah, where there was no work for him. Instead he ended up in Jaffa serving as a judge in the courts of the British Mandate. He disliked the English, although he liked the law. He continued living in Jaffa until 1948, when he, like the other inhabitants of the city, was forced out. He moved briefly with his family to Ramallah. During the first days they all stayed at Abu Ameen's house because it had thicker walls that they believed would better withstand bombardment from the air. But Saleem only managed to last a few days. He left his family with Abu Ameen and went to live alone in the summer house he owned up the hill, built from stones selected and cut by Abu Ameen. A month later he managed to leave Ramallah, where he never wanted to live. His cousin did not forgive him for this: 'He went and lived all by himself and left me with his difficult wife, Julia,' he used to complain. Saleem ended up in Beirut, a city by the sea like Jaffa, where he died alone.

Ayoub had stayed in Ramallah throughout Saleem's extensive travels. Everything took longer than he had anticipated. He had to work more years to make enough money to buy land. But then, in between the First World War and the end to Ottoman rule that followed, and the takeover of the country by the much different adminis-tration of the British Mandate, he succeeded. It was true the land he acquired wasn't as close to town as he would have wished, and it was not a very tempting plot, covered, as it was, with stones. But he knew how to clear it and turn it into cultivable land. He got married soon after he bought the property. He had not planned it this way: he had wanted first to finish building the *qasr*. Instead, on their honeymoon he took his bride to his newly bought property. They camped out in the open and, with no other help, the two of them managed the difficult feat of building the *qasr*. First they decided where it would sit. Then she cleared the ground, while he went looking for the right-sized stones. He said he needed big stones for the bottom rows. He would go in search of these and return carrying them clasped between his hands or supported on his shoulder. He was strong and as nimble as a goat, with short legs, a large muscular torso and a big chest, a hill man well adapted to this stony terrain. Zariefeh, his wife, was surely impressed with his physical strength. She had not expected it, for he was not tall. She would never have thought he would be able to handle all by himself the large rocks that he was bringing back to the construction site. He never complained and rarely took breaks. They worked well together, most of the time in silence. He was a quiet, serious man of few words. She did most of the talking. But when it came to stones, his skill was unrivalled. He only had to touch a stone to know what kind it was and whether or not it could take the weight.

Ordinarily the building of a *qasr* was a communal affair. The whole family joined in and together they could get it built in a matter of a few days. But Ayoub did not have that sort of family. His cousins were all useless. They wanted to study and after finishing school they left to pursue their education in the United States. He couldn't see the point of it. They deserted Ramallah as if it were not their town, their home, the place where they should strike roots, get married and bring up children as their fathers and forefathers had done. They all emigrated and left him alone in Ramallah.

What did he care? He knew his own strength and was confident of his abilities. He was an only child and now did not even have his cousins around him to help. But then he was used to depending on himself. And there was his wife to do what she could. Together they would build the *qasr* and make it one of the finest in the area.

On the first day they thought they would return to Ramallah at dusk but they lost themselves in the work and when they stopped the sun had already gone down. If they started back now they would have to walk in the dark and this was not safe because of the possibility of being attacked by jackals on the way. So they decided to stay on their land, and sleep the night. Ayoub went and fetched water from the spring. In her *zewadeh* Zariefeh had brought bread, white goat cheese, onions, dry figs and raisins. They put them down and ate. They had not planned on staying the night and so had not brought any canvas to cover themselves with. But they would be all right for tonight, there was no one around, they had the hills all to themselves. Ayoub made a fire to keep the jackals away and tried to stay awake as long as possible to watch over his young wife. But eventually he succumbed to sleep. When he woke up to a dewy, cool morning he thought he was in paradise. He loved being out in the hills. His young wife was next to him, they were on their own land – not confined inside a small space with the animals but outdoors in God's open country. He examined yesterday's work and saw how well Zariefeh had cleared the small plot and how he had begun laying out the foundation of the *qasr*. He went off to do his morning toilet out in the open without fear of anyone watching or coming along. He fetched more water and came back to find his wife awake.

They worked hard like this for six consecutive days. It was only because Zariefeh knew what was edible in the wild that they were able to survive in the hills on the provisions they had brought with them, thinking it was only going to be a day's excursion, not a full week. They rationed the bread and found some wild asparagus, watercress and thyme. In the evenings she prepared chamomile tea from the fresh herbs she found growing in the side of the hill. They ate and drank what they could collect and managed to keep hunger away, working continuously, stopping to rest only for brief intervals.

He was too shy at first to touch her in the open, it felt so exposed. But on the third day his desire was so strong it could not be contained. The *qasr* already had walls a metre and a half high. He felt that inside no one would be able to see them and, anyway, the possibility that someone should happen to pass by was surely remote. He also felt more comfortable sleeping behind these walls for an animal would not be able to leap in so easily and certainly not without bringing down some of the stones, which would make enough of a racket to wake him up.

And so the *qasr* was built entirely from stone without any cement. It was put together so well that it has lasted for well over half a century. It had a small door. When it was first built it had only one floor. But he had expected that he might have to enlarge it when his family grew. So he designed it with enough space for internal spiral stairs along the wall. In time he added another floor, making it a majestic, palatial *qasr* by any account, the highest and most spacious in the whole of the Ramallah hills.

I remember hearing when I was growing up how Abu Ameen had built the *qasr* with his wife on their honeymoon. We had all heard how, after they finished, he could not find anyone else around to do the *sakja* dance in celebration of the completion of the task. So he called on his wife: '*Yalla Ya*, Zariefeh.' She was a pretty woman and always wore a turban festooned with pierced Ottoman coins. She removed her turban, pulled up her *thob* (traditional Palestinian embroidered dress), took her husband's hand, and together they danced around their new home, until they fell to the ground with exhaustion. An expression relating to this became common in our family. When we had to do with less than what was normally required we would say: '*Yalla Ya*, Zariefeh' and get whoever was there to do it. I suspect that the description of the occasion as a honeymoon came later. When the couple were married I don't believe this concept existed. Couples had no leisure time at all. They were hard-nosed people who had little to survive on. What I marvel at is that in the midst of all this drudgery, Abu Ameen found the time to indulge himself and, using the skill he had learned carve out of stone his own *a'rsh*, a monument which has survived for some seventy-five years.

As I was growing up I heard a lot about the romanticized life of Abu Ameen – six months at home, six months in the hills. It was the subject of much talk. I never thought any of it was real. In my mind it was just family myth, folklore.

I also heard derogatory talk of the terrible time my family had when they stayed in his house. Naturally I only heard my parents' side of the story; how they took exception to the way Abu Ameen's family ate and behaved towards each other. But now I can imagine how he must have suffered. My family were judgemental, arrogant and proud of their education and status. They looked down on Abu Ameen and his family. 'What has he made of himself?' they would ask accusingly. 'Nothing, nothing at all. He was but a stonemason who sat under a rough canopy day in day out pecking at stone.'

It was true that at first Abu Ameen barely made enough money to survive and raise his large family. But after 1948, when Ramallah was swamped with refugees from the coastal towns in what became Israel, his fortunes changed. There was need for more housing and so Abu Ameen had more work. This meant that he was able to go less often on his *sarhat* to Harrasha and the place was neglected. All he could manage was to take care of the grapevines and the olive trees, doing the essential work of pruning and ploughing around their trunks in autumn after the harvest.

Then in 1955 disaster struck. The vines were afflicted by the deadly grape phylloxera for which there was then no known cure. The only way to stop its spread would have been to cut down all the vines in the way of the spread of the disease. But the farmers did not know this at the time; nor was anyone prepared to sacrifice his precious vines to save the whole crop. Everyone lost. The disease first hit the vines in the northern wadis, near Abu Ameen's land, then spread southward and eastward towards the town. In the course of a few years all the grapes that had made the hills around Ramallah green in spring and throughout the summer were gone. Only the hardy olive trees remained, seemingly eternal, planted in the midst of terraces that now had nothing else growing on them.

Abu Ameen looked with anger and despair at what was happening but did not have the means to put it right. After all his grapes died that summer he planned on putting in new seedlings during the next winter's planting season, but by the autumn of that year he had been afflicted by a stroke that left him lame and unable to farm. The dead vines in other plots were not replaced either, because many of the landowners were absent. They had emigrated in search of work to the Gulf or the United States and those who stayed had lost the hardiness which enabled the older generation to toil for little financial reward in the dry and stony hills of Ramallah.

I can barely remember the hills when the grapes draped their terrace walls. The custom was not to raise the stem of the vine off the ground but to lay it over the stone wall so that in summer the terraces became covered in green. Walking in the hills one can still see some of these stems, now charcoal black like amputated limbs strewn over the terrace stones. I must have been five years old when the process of their destruction by disease began. The house where I grew up overlooked the hills but I must have blocked out the memory of the shrivelling diseased vines. I remember my father regularly insisting that the best grapes were from the Ramallah hills. Everyone agreed.

When I was growing up, the hills for most of the year turned into dry, wild and distant places entangled with thistles and weeds, unvisited except by the shepherd boy with his sheep and goats. Shrubs grew everywhere unchecked. The terraces needed rehabilitation, parts of them having collapsed. The soil eroded as the retaining walls crumbled. Stones covered everything, washed over the soil where Abu Ameen and others used to plant. Many of the paths where he used to drive his mule were obliterated; left without cleaning, many springs had become clogged. The wadis now dried up long before the summer had even begun. The hills were an abandoned land and evidence of their neglect was apparent everywhere.

But in spring they were once again transformed with swathes of purple flax that could be glimpsed from afar, criss-crossed by different patterns of blue from the bugloss, clover and miniature iris like wafts of colour painted with a wide brush. In the early morning, as the droplets of dew clung to the delicate petals of the wild flowers catching the sunlight, the valleys seemed to glitter in a kaleidoscope of colour.

The outside of Abu Ameen's house in Ramallah had that fusty smell of laundry water spilt in the outside alley. In the small stone house with the thick walls, at the centre of the old town, with its large bell-shaped clay pot for keeping cool the drinking water which we called *El Zeer*, Abu and Um Ameen raised seven children, six boys and one girl. None were interested in education; nor did their parents encourage them. What their father desired for his children was that they would take up farming. But this was not to be. None of them were the least bit interested in even visiting Harrasha let alone farming it. They were all heavy smokers and found the walk there too arduous.

With ten people in that small two-room house, Abu Ameen's elderly mother included, Harrasha became even more important in the life of Abu Ameen. Every morning he emerged from the house feeling drowsy, close to being asphyxiated from the carbon monoxide fumes of the charcoal they burned on the small metal *qanoon* inside the house to keep warm. The toilet was outside the house and during cold winter nights the animals were brought inside and slept in the downstairs area. It was confined, stuffy and noisy. His cheeks would be flushed, his head so heavy that he would be surprised by the fresh air. He claimed he suffered headaches from the continuous chatter of the women. He could hardly wait for the end of winter so he could be out again in the hills, sleeping on the roof of his *qasr* under the starry night sky, waking up in the morning with his clothes wet from dew. It was the silence that he craved most of all. That unique silence of the hills where you could hear the slithering of a snake in the undergrowth.

He also looked forward to being away from the children. It was difficult to get them to work. All they wanted was to smoke and enjoy themselves. They didn't care about the land. They had a considerable plot behind the house, which he believed could be cultivated and turned into a paradise. But they were too lazy to do it. Out there in the hills he was oblivious to all his problems. He would not bother anyone; nor would there be anyone to bother him. If he did not wash and he smelled, no one would be around to complain. He would sleep and snore and no one could hear him and be annoyed. Nor did he have to put up with the snoring of the other members of his family or the animals. He didn't have to tell anyone what to do and fight with them if they didn't do it. There was no one to have to cajole, scold or argue with. Life on his own, with only the obedient mule around, was blissful.

All winter long he would wait for the weather to get

warmer, planning what he was going to accomplish in the spring when he went off to the hills. As soon as winter ended he loaded his mule with a *zewadeh* of provisions and rode away.

Once he got to his land he felt his year was beginning. His wasn't a large plot, but still there was much to be done and many rocks to clear.

This season he had big plans for his stay in the hills. First the essential jobs, the pruning and the ploughing; then he was going to make home improvements. He had in mind to carve a chair out of the rock that stood next to the door and was too big to remove. He wanted to turn it into the most comfortable seat possible, well proportioned with a good support to the lower back and with solid armrests, a real throne worthy of a king where he could sit alone after his work was done. Master of his own world, alone, happy and satisfied.

He worked constantly the entire day chiselling away at the rock. The chips flew all around him, the dust from the stone made his clothes, face and hair white like an old man's. He had a great capacity for work and he knew the material so well that every one of his blows was effective in shaping the rock the way he had planned. It was late in the afternoon when he finished. The sun was already setting and the wind had got up. He rested his weary body on the rock chair and was satisfied that it had all the right proportions, just as he had hoped. He looked around him and saw the beautiful *qasr* that he and his wife had built and the terracing of the land in front of it that was now finished and he felt that his happiness was complete.

Sometimes in the town he had his doubts about the way his life had proceeded. These were especially strong when his cousin Saleem visited from Jaffa. In Harrasha he looked forward to his cousin's visits, but not when he came to Ramallah in winter. Then Saleem would be wearing a three-piece suit and wire-rimmed spectacles, and smoking a pipe. Abu Ameen believed it was too much reading that had spoiled his cousin's eyes. He himself had eyes like a hawk and never needed to wear glasses. Saleem now considered himself a *Yaffawi* (someone who comes from Jaffa). He even owned a hotel in the city, the Continental. He read big books in English but didn't stop complaining about the *Engleez*. He sat awkwardly on one of the low chairs while the rest of them sat on the floor around him. He looked as though he was presiding over everyone, as if he were a judge also here in the humble house. He never talked about how Abu Ameen had not moved from the village where he began his life, never even leaving the house where he was born, but his silence said it all. It was as though he was constantly saying: 'Look at me. I have made something of myself, left Ramallah, got educated. And you are still ignorant, wearing your *qumbaz*, looking like your father. You're no improvement whatsoever.'

But now in the hills all such doubt vanished. He was sure of himself, sure that he was as happy as any man could be. Why should he exchange his comfortable *qumbaz* for a restrictive Western suit? Any time he wanted to relieve himself he just found a stone, and there were plenty of them around. He would squat raising his garment and do it. No need for the fuss which his cousin would have to go through with his long trousers and jacket. The air was constantly circulating between his legs. He could feel it; it was nourishing and refreshing. Why would anyone want to wrap oneself in a garment that would keep him hot all summer? Just to look like the *Engleez*? What does he care about them? What are they to him anyway?

How far he felt from everything objectionable. The *Engleez* never came here. He would have the entire six months in the hills and never see a single one of them. Why would they come? They were not interested in these hills. They are not for them. They lived in cities, they wouldn't be able to manage here. They were too refined, delicate, spoiled. His cousin was becoming like them, he had even begun to speak like them, hardly moving his lips. And instead of rolling his own cigarettes he was constantly busy with his pipe, taking it out of his mouth, putting it back in, pushing it to the corner of his mouth as he looked sideways, as though he was calculating, judging.

While Abu Ameen was involved in his own affairs, cultivating his orchard, oblivious to the rest of the world, the worst war in human history was taking place. The Nazis were massacring the Jews and the gypsies and the calls for a Jewish state were growing stronger. Saleem, who was an avid reader of the papers, local and international, had already formulated his own opinions on world affairs. He also had his own predictions about the dismal future of Palestine. The iron determination of the Zionists coupled with Palestine's ineffective local leadership alarmed him.

When they happened to discuss these matters Abu Ameen argued strongly that this was none of his business. None of these affairs meant anything to his family because they were from Ramallah. He saw his life as beginning and ending in a place where no one ever encountered Jews or saw any of their much-talked-about settlements. His cousin was bringing ruin on his head by meddling in what was none of his business.

Here in these hills, sitting on his throne he was emperor, the unrivalled king. He thought of his cousin travelling to America, of his bragging about how he camped out on the deck of the ship. Oh how often he heard him repeat this story. The others in his household loved to hear him tell it and would ask him to repeat it every time he visited. What's the big deal in sleeping on the deck and having to work in the galley to pay for his fare? He sleeps out in the open all summer long and no one thinks much of it; how is it different to sleep on the deck of the ship? And yet to be on the open sea. Not to be able to see any land for months, how strange it must be. No, it was not for him, not for him.

He belonged here, why pretend otherwise? This was his home, where he belonged and where he would remain until his dying day. This was his world and it was a world he preferred to any other.

Abu Ameen was able to look out on the hills that remained unchanged throughout his life except for the disappearance of the grapevines. He could not have been aware how fortunate he was to have had the security and comfort of seeing the same unaltered view of the hills. I was born among hills that looked more or less as they did during the last years of Abu Ameen's life. But throughout my adult life I had the misfortune of witnessing their constant transformation. I first learned of the Israeli government's settlement plans through the research I did for the human rights organization, Al Haq, that I co-directed. What I read was cause enough for concern.

But, I wondered, would it really be possible to implement these plans? Could our hills, unchanged for centuries, become home within a matter of a few years for around 100,000 Jewish settlers who claim a divine right to them, who ultimately want to drive us away? The hills which had provided the setting for tranquil walks where I felt more freedom than I did anywhere else in the world would eventually become confining, endangered areas and a source of constant anxiety.

One hilltop after another was claimed as more and more Jewish settlements were established. Then the settlements were joined with each other to form 'settlement blocs'. Roads were built between these clusters and ever-expanding areas of land around them were reserved for their future growth, depriving more villages of the agricultural land they depended upon for their livelihood. Thus one bloc of settlements was created north of Ramallah, another to the east and many more to the south. And between the blocs to the east smaller settlements called outposts began to crop up so that when I looked at night towards the north I saw a continuous stretch of settlements and roads that were creating a noose around Ramallah. Then to make matters worse a 670-kilometre wall was planned, across the West Bank, that would further divide Ramallah from the villages surrounding it, complicating our life immeasurably and causing yet greater damage to our beautiful landscape.

How I envy Abu Ameen his confidence and security in the hills where he was born and died, which he believed would remain unchanged for ever. Could Abu Ameen have ever dreamed that one day the open hills to which he escaped the confinement of life in the village would be out of reach for his descendants? How unaware many trekkers around the world are of what a luxury it is to be able to walk in the land they love without anger, fear or insecurity, just to be able to walk without political arguments running obsessively through their heads, without the fear of losing what they've come to love, without the anxiety that they will be deprived of the right to enjoy it. Simply to walk and savour what nature has to offer, as I was once able to do.

Abu Ameen died when I was only six. His wife, Zariefeh, held on for much longer. Of her six sons and one daughter, one left for Central America and was never heard of again. Another, the eldest, was amongst the first from Ramallah to begin working on the oil rigs of the Arabian Gulf, where the temperature in the summer reached over 50°C and where there was still no air conditioning. He worked in catering and would pass through Beirut on his way home and spend most of the money he had made in the arduous and sweltering environment of the oil-rich Gulf. He was one of the most generous men I knew. In time he took two of his younger brothers to work with the same company. But the brothers could not work together. They were too individualistic, and they constantly quarrelled. Neither could they stand the bossiness of their elder brother. One of them emigrated to the United States and the other found work in Kuwait, but he did not last long there. The heat was too much for him and he yearned for the cool Ramallah weather. 'My father died when I was away,' he told his wife. 'I don't want the same to happen to my mother.' His wife, who had been hoping for a better life and had found a job in Kuwait, was dismayed. She did not want to return to be with his mother in the old house in the old city. I remember her when we went to welcome them back, sitting forlornly in a corner of the crowded old house with red-rimmed eyes and tears rolling down her pale cheeks. She blew her nose with rolls of soft paper that I had never seen before. I remember having the sinking feeling that this tissue now wet with her tears was all she had managed to bring back with her from the country where many had made their fortune.

And then there was Salameh, the youngest brother. He worked with glass, framing pictures. I would often come for the lunch break from school and find him there at my grandmother's house. It never occurred to me that a young man spending so much time outside his shop must not have much work. Then one day he began speaking about *hujra* (emigration). My grandmother tried to tell him all the bad things about the United States, she being the only member of the family who had travelled there to visit her son. 'It's not as you think, gold in the streets ready to be picked,' she said. She would boast: 'I crossed the Atlantic four times, I should know.'

When Zariefeh died none of her seven children were around except Ameen. He had been sent for at the last minute and managed to arrive from the Gulf before she let go. But he was so sentimental and sad that the only way he could endure her passing was by drinking heavily. By the time she gave up the ghost he was so inebriated that he had to be carried to her funeral. With Um Ameen's death the eldest member of our extended family was gone, a venerable, strong woman who spent the last few years of her life unwell, with her complexion becoming darker and darker, and her eyes losing their spark as the cancer consumed her liver. She was the last of the women in our family to wear the *thob*, the traditional dress, colourfully embroidered, with the head turban festooned with Ottoman coins.

After his mother's death Ameen could no longer motivate himself to return to his job in the Gulf. He decided to emigrate to the United States like his brothers. I remember my grandmother saying that with him gone none of our many close relatives would be left behind. She tried her best to dissuade him from emigrating to the extent of warning him sternly that his wife, who had a dark complexion, would be taken for a woman of colour, 'and they don't treat such people well in America,' adding 'they follow them in the streets and mock them and sometimes they even shoot them.' The way she put it made me wonder how on earth Ameen could consider emigrating when he would be risking the life of his wife.

These warnings didn't work. The couple emigrated anyway. Once in the US they worked day and night and made good money. Their children learned to speak English like American kids on television with that slur and intonation that made them sound foreign to their parents, not at all like the kids they had given birth to in Ramallah. When their parents addressed them in Arabic they refused to answer. They pleaded with them not to embarrass them before their friends. The children adjusted all too well to American society. But not their parents, who finished their days in dark rooms, silent and depressed, thinking only of the homeland to which the state of Israel would not allow them to return. None of the seven children, and their forty descendants, of Abu Ameen, who created Harrasha, were left in Ramallah. Of Saleem's descendants, I and my brother, Samer, are the only two still living here.

෫ඵ

In the spring of 2003, many years after I first discovered Harrasha, I decided to take my nephew, Aziz, Samer's ten-year-old son, to show him his ancestor's *qasr* and to have him sit on the *a'rsh*.

The Second Intifada, which began in September 2000, had led to an increase in internal migration into Ramallah from other West Bank cities such as Nablus and Jenin, where Israeli policies had made life unbearable. The city became one of the few in the West Bank with a mixed population of Christians and Muslims originating from the various regions of Palestine. It also became the unnamed capital of the Palestinian Authority, housing the seat of the Palestinian Legislative Council, the executive offices of the President of the Palestinian Authority and the High Court of Justice. But all these developments came at a price. As the city's population expanded more land was needed for housing. The wild and beautiful hills surrounding it began to be invaded, not only by the Jewish settlements which were being established all around its wide periphery, but also by the insatiable appetite of the city's inhabitants for expansion and growth.

The Palestinian police, established after the Oslo Accords, built its headquarters behind the Anglican school close to the starting point of my walks in the hills. This hexagonal structure was topped by a dome painted lemon yellow emulating the now unreachable Dome of the Rock in Jerusalem, twelve kilometres away. Its discordant profile continued to dominate this part of the hills until the early years of the Intifada, when it was demolished by a one-ton bomb dropped by an Israeli F16 fighter jet.

Aziz and I walked around the bombed-out police station to get to Harrasha. He was excited about the prospect of seeing the *qasr* and the *a'rsh* about which I had long spoken to him, so we walked as fast as possible, taking the most direct route to get to it. When we arrived we found the *qasr* intact but some dull-witted stone thief must have tried to excavate the *a'rsh*, perhaps to take it to his garden or sell it. He had not realized that it was carved out of such a massive rock that it was impossible to remove. But in the course of his ill-conceived attempt he had managed to topple Abu Ameen's *a'rsh* on its side, rendering it unusable.

Aziz was disappointed. The *a'rsh* had been desecrated and displaced, becoming just another of the many rocks dispersed over the side of the hill. It was impossible to explain to my nephew how it had looked in its former glory standing straight, its large base buried in the earth. Or how good it felt to sit on it. It was now robbed of that magic which I had tried to describe when I convinced him to take the long risky trip with me through the hills.

We visited the *qasr*, using the spiral stairs to go up and stand on top looking out at the hills. But this was no compensation. Aziz had set his mind on sitting in the *a'rsh* as I had promised. We tried to return to Ramallah using a different route, hoping to find something exciting on the way that would compensate for the disappointment and take his mind off it. We ended up by the demolished police station, which Aziz said he was curious to inspect. We trudged slowly through a field speckled with the carcasses of destroyed cars, garbage, rubble, mangled metal, aluminium, pieces of yellow concrete, glass and parts of bombs and spent bullets, the detritus of years of neglect, dashed hopes, resistance and war.

Aziz wanted to run ahead in the ruts made by Israeli tanks that had come to inspect the bombed-out area. I walked one terrace below. I was continuing my search for the old path amidst the transformed hill when I heard him calling. I lifted my head and saw that he was holding up a long thick tube made of metal. 'What is this?' he asked. It didn't immediately occur to me that Aziz had picked up part of an unexploded missile. He stood there with the sun shining behind him, waiting for my answer. A moment of panic seized me and I felt myself going numb, deadened by the dreadful prospect of seeing my nephew explode before my eyes. Slowly but emphatically I said: 'Keep holding it. Do not throw it,' and I began moving steadily towards him. He must have heard the dread in my voice for he froze on the spot. When I got to him I eased the object from his hands, held on to it and told him to run. My heart was pounding but I was ecstatic to see my nephew escape a lethal explosion. Slowly I placed the object on the ground and whispered a quiet prayer.

Sometimes when I wake up early and look from my house at the hills, I imagine Abu Ameen standing in the morning on the roof of his *qasr* deep in the hills. He is drowned in the mist which has filled the valley and obliterated the folds of the hills, smoothing them out. Around him I can see how it has settled in every nook and crevice of the valley, creating numerous steamy lakes in the dry, baked hills. He remains standing in this transformed landscape, following the sun's ascent in the sky, observing it suck up the mist, empty the nocturnal lakes and return the undulating hills to their usual parched state.

If someone were looking for Abu Ameen from afar he would not at first be able to make him out. Then as the mist began to lift and the sun grew stronger, a luminous figure would start to emerge. The wisps of vapour surrounding him would light up with the sun. Iridescent sparks would illuminate his body, giving him wings with which he could soar over the valleys, an ephemeral figure like a wild fowl or a pale god of the hills.

I have often wondered about Abu Ameen as I stand in the early morning looking over the countryside. What would he have said had he seen the state they were now in? Would his spirit be brimming with anger at all of us for allowing them to be destroyed and usurped, or would he just be enjoying one extended *sarha* as his spirit roamed freely over the land, without borders as it had once been?

2

THE ALBINA CASE

Ramallah to A'yn Qenya

For the first two decades of the Israeli occupation of the West Bank I was still able to walk in the hills unhampered. Although a large number of settlements had been established in various parts of the land, the number of settlers living on our side of the border was small. We still believed that it was possible for the occupation to end one day and for peace to be established on the basis of the creation of a Palestinian state in the West Bank alongside Israel. But the changes that the Israeli military authorities were carrying out to the laws on the administration of land were worrisome. I was following them with deep concern.

One day in 1979 I went to the Land Registration Department in Ramallah, as I often did at that time, to check the details of a client's property. The usual crowds waiting at the door were not there. The place looked deserted. I knocked and waited. Eventually Ghazi, the Land Registrar, opened the door and asked, as though surprised to see me, what I wanted. I told him I needed to check the Land Register.

'You can't,' he said.

'Why not?' I asked.

'New instructions,' he answered.

'Then perhaps you can check it for me.'

'No chance,' he said. 'We are all very busy. We have orders to make a survey of the different types of land and it is taking a lot of time. No one can help you today, perhaps not tomorrow either, not even in a few weeks.'

Until then the records of the Land Registration Department controlled by the Israeli military government and its 'civil' administration were open for inspection by the public as they had been under Jordanian rule. Since that day in 1979 they have been out of reach, secret. The Israeli official responsible for the Palestinian Land Authority, with the help of his Palestinian employees, was conducting a survey of the types of land to determine what percentage was registered and what sort of registration documentation existed. This information was vital for the success of the settlement project and it was carefully guarded. Since that day the Palestinian public have been denied access to the land records.

I went back to the office and applied myself to preparing the summation of the Albina land case. I was contesting before an Israeli court, a declaration by the Israeli Custodian of Public and Absentee Property on land in the village of Beit 'Ur near Ramallah. I thought this would take the whole day. But before noon I had finished and decided to go back home. I had to walk because my brother had borrowed my car. When I got there I found that I did not have the key to my house. It was with my car keys. I had forgotten to take it off when I gave Samer the car.

I sat on the steps leading to the garden and considered what I should do next. It had been a tiring morning. I so much wanted to go inside and relax. My house was a small two-room structure which I had rented three years earlier, a simple structure with a small garden that had a fig tree growing out of the rocks, shading the side entrance which I used as the main door. The room where I slept and worked had one window overlooking the garden. It was not a particularly charming house and it got very cold in winter. I had chosen it because of its proximity to the hills.

I had not left these two rooms that last weekend. I had shut myself up in the house, writing and listening to the rain thumping down on my roof. I got such a sense of relief from hearing the water pouring down from the heavens, running down the pipes to the cistern situated close to the fig tree. During the winter months when it doesn't rain I get anxious. I begin to feel something is terribly amiss. Then when the rain returns a feeling of well-being comes over me. This was a good house in which to listen to the falling rain. Could this obsession with rain be related to a primordial anxiety passed on from my ancestors, who depended on agriculture for their livelihood? Living in a dry land which gets all its water from the few months of winter rain must have ingrained a fear of drought deep within me, though I've never experienced one myself. What other hidden fears do I have, fears I'm forever trying to discover so that I can free myself from them? How I have thought of becoming free! But are my endeavours futile?

Perhaps the paucity of rain is what makes us, the inhabitants of this land, Jews and Arabs, so anxious and temperamental that peace continues to elude us. It was here that prophets thought they heard God imposing punishment by withholding the rain or rewarding His people with fertile fields. Such a small land with an outstanding variety of topographies, one snow-capped mountain, which belongs to Syria, one desert, one fresh-water lake and another very salty one, and one proper river. One of everything. And so little water that we've had to live with our eyes constantly turned up to the heavens.

The previous night, after several days of heavy showers, the rain had stopped. The heavens cleared to show a fresh turquoise sky. It was much too beautiful a day to wish to be indoors. What was I waiting for? I had my book. I didn't need any special clothing or shoes to walk in these hills. I simply turned up my trouser legs to avoid muddying them and thought I would walk to the enormous pine tree midway down the hill and read. There weren't many pines in the hills. I didn't know who had planted this one or whether it had seeded itself. I often took my book and went there to sit and read. When I returned home my brother would have brought back my car. He would put the keys underneath the loose tile to the left of the door, as agreed.

I was expecting the path to be still muddy but found that the surface soil had dried and it was soft to walk on without being sticky. Built many years ago by the owners of the land, the path was a few metres wide and bordered on each side by stone walls. It sloped gently along the side of the hill then turned and headed downhill. It had been carefully designed. Had it followed a straight line down it would be washed out in winter, unusable, more a canal for water than a footpath.

When I got to where the path began to turn downhill, I jumped over the terrace wall and walked a few metres to where the pine tree to which I was headed stood. As

I brushed aside its needles, a whiff of the familiar pine odour hit me. I entered the fragrant cavern created by the branches of this fifty-year-old tree. It was dim inside, for the tree shaded the sun. It was most unlikely that this tree had been cultivated. No farmer worthy of the name would have planted it here. It had no function and only made the soil acidic. A seed must have been blown accidentally with the wind or transported unintentionally by some hapless farmer, getting stuck in the folds of his clothes and then, as he passed here on his way to check on his olives, had fallen to the ground.

Ordinarily I would sit on the ground leaning my back against the low-lying trunk, facing east, listening to the soft susurration of the branches and read. But today the soil was too wet and I had nothing to cover the ground with. I straddled the trunk, resting my back on a branch. Rather than read, I took in the view. What a different air this tree gave to these hills, I thought, as I sat surrounded by its drooping branches looking out at the landscape.

Now that I was thinking of pines I noticed many more were growing between the olive trees on the facing hill. All it took was for one tree to establish roots. Then when it seeded, its cones would open, spreading seeds from terrace to terrace, multiplying the pines at the expense of those trees that had been there long before them. Much as I liked pine trees they looked like intruders, evidence of the abandonment of these hills to the forces of nature. They were dark green in colour as opposed to the blue-green of the olive trees, and they grew tall and large and tried to claim the land where they struck root, imposing themselves on the hills. Like the olive trees their roots remained close to the surface, knotted and smoothed like knuckles, scrambling for the same piece of ground, making it hard for them to coexist.

We were between storms; another was expected in a few days, a cold front from the north. For now the sky was that turquoise visible in the waters of the Dead Sea on clear days. When it was not cloudy, the clarity of the air during these winter months made it possible to see all the way to the Mediterranean, the clear blue-green sea winking beyond the hills.

I had intended to sit under the pine tree and read but the sight of the hills spread out before me clear and fresh with the olive trees washed with the rain, and the splashes of green here and there accented by the blooming bulbs, made me want to get down to the valley and see more. I slipped my book in my pocket and was on my way.

Once the ways of these hills were known only to those who used them. They could tell which land was whose and roughly where the borders of each plot lay. Then in 1865 the first preliminary meeting of the Society of the Palestine Exploration Fund, established 'for the purpose of investigating the Archaeology, Geography, Geology and Natural History of the Holy Land', was held in the Jerusalem Chamber of the Palace of Westminster. The original prospectus of the Society declared that:

> No country should be of so much interest to us as that in which the documents of our Faith were written, and the momentous events they describe enacted. At the same time no country more urgently requires illustration. ... Even to a casual traveller in the Holy Land the Bible becomes, in its form, and therefore to some extent in its substance, a new book. Much would be gained by ... bringing to light the remains of so many races and

generations which must lie concealed under the accu-
mulation of rubbish and ruins on which those villages
stand ...

Thus began a process that continues to this day of travellers and colonizers who see the land through the prism
of the biblical past, overlooking present realities. Eager
to occupy the land of their imagination they impose
their vision and manipulate it to tally with that mythical
image they hold in their head, paying scant notice to its
Palestinian inhabitants.

From 1882 to 1888 the Palestine Exploration Fund sent
its cartographers to prepare survey maps. The hills began
to witness men from other lands with funny instruments
and hats. Among them were those who could speak the
local language, who asked the locals about the names of
places. The locals obliged. The British wanted to know the
name of every hillock, every wadi, every spring. Knowledge
is power. A prerequisite for successful conquest, which
came some years later, is for the conquering army to
know the ways of the land, its features, its secrets, its
names. A third party came between the people and their
land. All this pre-dated the British Mandate.

Europe, and later Zionism, has endeavoured to rescue
the historical significance of the region in its search for
ancient Israel: a search for its own cultural roots which
in the process has silenced Palestinian history and
relegated it to prehistory, paving the way for the modern
state of Israel to take control not only of the land but
also of Palestinian time and space. Unlike Jerusalem,
Jericho, Nablus and Hebron, Ramallah was fortunate,
amongst West Bank cities, in escaping any mention in
the Bible. It was a parvenu village, historically and reli-

giously insignificant. How I rejoice at this omission. We have our Jewish settlements on the outskirts but at least we have been spared the terror of fanatic fundamentalists squatting inside our town claiming that it belongs to their ancestors on biblical grounds as has happened in the old city of Hebron.

In 1888 the Palestine Exploration Fund produced scale maps of Palestine of 1:100,000. These were the basis for land registration, which began half a century later during the British Mandate period and continued under Jordan in 1955. It was suspended by Israel after it occupied the West Bank in 1967.

Land registration operations covered all the hills to the south-west of Ramallah, including the village of Beit 'Ur, where the land of my client, Albina, on whose case I was working that morning, is situated. But in this area the very last step in the protracted process could not take place. The Schedule of Rights was prepared and signed in Amman, Jordan, where, until 1967, the headquarters of the Land Department were situated. The Schedule then had to be brought back to Ramallah, where the results would be entered in the local register and the process made absolutely final. The war that started on 5 June 1967 prevented this from taking place. The exact borders of Albina's land were delineated on a map and given a number but the Certificate of Registration could not be issued. This formality was the loophole the settlers used to question my client's ownership of his land.

I followed the path quickly as if I was running away. What was I running from? I didn't stop until the path meandered once again to the right, going in the direction of the next village. There were some large exposed rocks there, a good place to stop and catch my breath. I was already too far down to see the town or to be seen. How often I had come to these hills as a younger man running away from the eyes of my parents and the rest of society. Living as I did in a stifling community these hills were my only escape, as they had been to Abu Ameen. I could now slow down, rest on this rock and look at the wide valley of Wadi El 'qda ('the knot') and the open hillside opposite. I squatted and felt the gentle cool breeze against my face. For the first time that day I breathed deeply and enjoyed the clean air filling my lungs.

In between the stones there was a shiny, almost wispy layer of grass embossed with droplets of water that glistened in the sun. The lichen-covered rocks made the trickling water look black. The afternoon sun cast long shadows from the olive trees. Amongst the green grass and winter flowers there was a predominance of dark green, black and charcoal.

The thistles and shrubs burned from last summer's heat mixed with the soil and were wet. Amongst them were a few surviving twigs of sage from last year's bushes. I pinched one between my fingers and enjoyed its strong aroma. The earth was variegated with dark spots between the green and the grey stones. The green went up over the bulky roots of the trees around their thick trunks. There were blue hyacinth squills between the rocks. When I slid down and stood again on the path I noticed the crocuses that had sprung out after the rain, filling the little patch around the rock I was sitting on like a pink haze. I didn't want to crush their delicate petals so close to the ground but this was unavoidable for they were everywhere.

Because of my work and the heavy rain, which made the path too muddy, I hadn't been able to walk all last week. This was what accounted for my tense state. Walking helped me put things in perspective. I now began to pick up pace and hurried down the sloping path towards the wadi. The further down I went the deeper the silence. As always the distance and quiet made me attentive to those troublesome thoughts that had been buried deep in my mind. As I walked many of them were surfacing. I sifted through them. The mind only admits what it can handle and here on these hills the threshold was higher.

The other day I had to plead with a soldier to be allowed to return home. I was getting back from our winter house in Jericho, where I had spent a relaxing day. I had to implore the Israeli soldier. I told him that I really did not know curfew had been imposed on Ramallah. I was away all day and hadn't listened to the news. 'I'm tired,' I said, 'please let me through.' Oh the humiliation of pleading with a stranger for something so basic. Why should I endure all these hardships? Why should I spend so much of my time thinking about the dismal future? Living as a hunted, haunted human with a terrible sense of doom pervading my life? Why could I not live the moment, be at ease? But I knew why. If I and people like me were to leave rather than stay and resist the occupation, we would wake up in a few years to a new reality, with our land taken from under our feet. We had no alternative but to struggle against our predicament.

As long as there were no Israeli settlements nearby I could pretend that I had the whole of the hills to myself. A silent arena. The path I was on had once connected the villages north of Ramallah to those in the south. Many must have walked these same paths, not for pleasure but for work, transporting produce and commuting from village to village. This had been the only way to move around before the paved roads were opened. Only recently did I learn from a friend that even these very paths I've been using on my walks are marked on a British-made Ordnance map. I had wanted to believe this was my path, known only to me, my own discovery, that these hills were my private arena where I could be alone. I looked up the Mandate maps and found that my friend was right. The path was marked. It stretched from A'yn Arik, a village west of Ramallah, all the way down to the Mediterranean Sea.

Normally, when I only had time for a short walk, I would continue straight down and once in the valley I would turn around and walk back up. Today I had more time. Rather than continue down, I decided to head northwards, traversing the hill I was on and going down into the next gully. The further away from town I moved the less cultivated were the fields, until I got to a hill that was covered with weeds. Here and there, hanging down from the stone terraces, I could see dead charcoal-black branches, remnants of the once vibrant grapevines that had filled these hills, cascading down over the terrace walls. I stopped to examine them. I could smell their damp rot.

Most of the rocks here are limestone, sedimentary rock formed under the deep sea that once covered these hills. I often found fossils of different shellfish. On my desk at home I have several fossilized snails. Only on this side of the Great Fault can sea fossils be found. On the east side of the River Jordan, where the shallow edge of the ancient sea was, there is only terrestrial sandstone and grit.

Nearby I noticed a number of strange-looking rocks. I knelt down to examine them more closely. Protruding out of them like a relief were tube-like fossilized roots. I picked up another, the size of my palm, which was stuffed in the terrace wall. I noticed it because it was the colour of the brown soil, unlike the grey rocks used to build the wall. I held it in my hand and examined it closely. I was amazed. It looked as though hundreds of shells of sea snails, starfish and sea urchins had been pressed together to form this small grooved rock. Lithification is the general term for a group of processes that convert loose sediment into rock. Most sediments are lithified by a combination of compaction, which packs loose cement grains tightly together, and cementation, in which the precipitation of a cement around the grains binds them into a firm hard rock. This rock must have been millions of years old, from when this area was submerged under the sea.

I had ventured into a fascinating area. Not far from the terrace wall, tall as an altar, I saw a large rock that seemed out of place as though it had fallen from on high. It was cracked in a number of places. I rested my elbows on it and examined it more closely. The sun was striking it at a thirty-degree angle. Engraved in the rock were two elongated lobes, one on each side, with a long mound like a giant toe between them. The whole thing was over a metre in length. At first I thought these shapes must have been made by water running down the rock over many years. But why would the water make circular grooves? I had once seen pictures of dinosaur footprints; the similarity here was striking. I lifted my eyes and tried to imagine an enormous animal standing with one foot over this rock, its head almost reaching the top of the hill overlooking Ramallah. How brief a moment is given to us to be here on earth. And how beautiful was that moment then with the hills all spread out before me, not submerged under water, not dominated by enormous animals, but full of wonderful treasures.

Before moving away from this rock I made sure to remember its location: several terraces down from the pine trees, halfway between the top of the hill and the valley, in a field full of the common thistle called *natsh* (Poterium Thorn), which was likely used to make the crown of thorns worn by Christ. *Natsh* is as plentiful in these hills as heather in the Scottish Highlands. Both are tenacious plants with strong roots. In winter *natsh* acquires thick narrow leaves that conserve water. The fields are full of small green mounds not unlike porcupines. As the dry summer months advance the leaves eventually dry up and fall off, leaving humps of wiry mesh that farmers sometimes cut and use as a broom to clean coarse surfaces of pebbles and stone. It is also used to drain water and, because of its elasticity, as a substitute for a spring mattress by people who are sleeping out in the open. In Arabic the verb *natasha* means to pluck, hence the name of the weed extractor, *Minttash*. In Israeli military courts this weed has gained great popularity. Never has a weed been more exploited and politicized, not least by Dani Kramer, the legal advisor to the Israeli military government responsible for expropriating Palestinian land for Jewish settlements.

Dani's eyes would pop out if he should visit this hill. He knew few Arabic words. *Natsh* was one of them. How often have I heard him stand up before the judge in the military land court and declare: 'But, Your Honour, the land is full of *natsh*. I saw it with my own eyes.' Meaning: what more proof could anyone want that the land was uncultivated and therefore public land that the Israeli settlers could use as their own?

The other hero of the settlement project, whom I had heard a lot about but never met, was Rabbi Kook. He once described to his disciples how his identification with the land was so total that he felt his own body torn. It was not clear whether or not the land in question was replete with *natsh*. Surely not! He was speaking metaphorically of much more profound things. It was the night of 14 May 1967, just before the war that resulted in the occupation of the Palestinian territories, the eve of Israel's Independence Day and the anniversary of the UN resolution that gave the state its legal standing. As he delivered his sermon he began to shout and his body was rocked by grief. He was recalling the announcement in 1947, twenty years earlier, when the UN decided to partition Palestine into a Jewish and an Arab state. While the Jews in Palestine danced in the streets, the rabbi sat alone bewailing the division of the land. He asked his disciples: 'Where is Hebron? Have we forgotten it? And where is our Shkehm [Nablus]? And our Jericho – will we forget them? And the far side of Jordan – it is ours, every clod of soil ... every region and bit of earth belonging to the lord's land. Is it in our hands to give up even a millimetre? In that state,' he said, 'my entire body shaking, entirely wounded and cut to pieces, I could not celebrate.' When I read this I thought: God help us. But for now I was not going to think any more of Rabbi Kook and his body, or of Dani and his legal fetish for *natsh*. I was going to enjoy my walk.

The final section of the path that brought me down to the valley was narrow and overgrown with spiky shrubs. I forced my way through, scratching my skin until the path veered to the right. The walls diverged. I continued on the open path parallel to the valley. I was fanned by the soft breeze that was blowing across this open green area. To my left stretched tall grass and olive trees luxuriating in the deep rich soil. I walked along, passing the gully between the next two hills. The valley here was at its widest. Winding their way between the terraces were flocks of sheep roaming on the sides of the hills like yellow ribbons. I looked for the shepherd and saw that he was just getting ready to play his reed pipe. I stopped in my tracks, sat on a rock and listened to his pastoral tunes. Then I began walking again, trying to move as quietly as possible.

I soon got to that part of the wadi which always inspired talk when I walked with Jonathan Kuttab, my colleague in human rights at Al Haq in 1981. Far away from town, next to the dry stream between the hills, we would sit on the rock, our feet dangling in the grass. Jonathan was thinking of getting married. We discussed his prospects. We talked of what lay ahead for us. We had both read the settlement master plan drawn up by the Jewish Regional Council in the West Bank in cooperation with the Settlement Department of the World Zionist Organization. According to this plan 80,000 Israeli Jews were to be settled in our hills by 1986 in twenty-five settlements and twenty outposts. To make this possible two billion US dollars were to be allocated. Tons of concrete were to be poured over these hills. The plan called for paving roads at a rate of 150 kilometres a year. Every year over 500 dunums (a dunum is 1,000 sq metres) of industrial zones would be developed. All the available natural resources would be monopolized by these settlers. 'Settlement blocs' would spread over the entire area and our towns and villages would be isolated, their growth hindered by a massive road network.

The plan viewed our presence here as a constraint and aimed at preventing our 'undesirable development'. By creating new human settlements where none existed, connecting them with roads, and isolating existing ones, it would not only strangle our communities but also destroy this beautiful land, and in a matter of a few years change what had been preserved for centuries. Ariel Sharon, the then Defense Minister, declared: 'We are going to leave an entirely different map of the country that it will be impossible to ignore.' Menachem Begin, the Prime Minister at the time, announced: 'Settlement [in the occupied areas] is the soul of Zionism.' The Israeli newspapers reported that the government in Israel had asserted that it would never accept dividing the Greater Land of Israel, never agree to the establishment of a Palestinian state between the River Jordan and the Mediterranean Sea. We were certain that we could not remain idle in the face of this existential threat. We had to do everything we could to resist it. If the plan should be implemented generations of young Jewish kids would grow up in our hills considering them their home and we would have another hundred years of struggle over this part of Palestine. As we sat on the rock in the Wadi 'qda Jonathan and I proceeded to formulate our legal struggle against the Israeli plan.

The olive trees at the bottom of this wadi stood in flat, freshly tilled soil. We considered this the midway point of our walk, after which we would begin our ascent back to Ramallah. We ate apples as we discussed the future of the legal struggle. We plotted how through legal action we were going to frustrate the whole of the Israeli settlement project. We would raise money for legal aid to challenge every land expropriation order and put a stop to this charade which claimed the settlers were only taking land that belonged to no one.

As Jonathan and I talked, I looked around. I was fond of the rocks here, with the grass bunching up around them. They looked as though they had burst out of the ground, small islands perched on a sea of green. The hills spread before us, leaning back comfortably, creating a wider valley. The ruin of an old collapsed *qasr* stood to our right. In winter, when the water seeped down from the hills it drained into a narrow channel between the rocks. The path ran by its side. More flowers would bloom here than anywhere else in the hills.

We were aware that the main argument the Israeli military was using was that non-registered land in the West Bank was public land. This could be used to settle Israeli Jews. The implications were calamitous. According to this interpretation of the land law, the only non-registered land that truly belonged to Palestinians was that over which they could prove use either by living on it or continuously cultivating it for a period of not less than ten years. All the rest was public land. This would render Palestinians living in the West Bank squatters, not rightful owners. The only rightful owners, according to the Israeli government's version of law and history, were the Jews, who could trace their entitlement to the land from time immemorial, just after the dinosaurs became extinct. Legally this position was not sustainable. And yet it was not being challenged. Most Palestinians boycotted Israeli courts, where these challenges could be presented. The settlers could comfort themselves that they were not taking anyone's private land to establish their settlements.

Jonathan, with his Afro hairstyle, bright white teeth

and long fingers, stressed every word. His eyes would widen when he wanted to emphasize a point, black intelligent eyes that sparkled. 'We must challenge these claims,' he announced, speaking loudly for all the hills to hear. 'We know what is right. We must not make it easy for Israel to take our land. We'll bring hundreds, thousands, of cases before their courts until we exhaust their system. Can you see it, going to Nurit at the military court with boxes of claims and seeing her surprise at this barrage of new cases that she has to process? I love it. I feel so excited by the prospect.'

We did not lose enthusiasm after we completed our walk. Al Haq established a special legal aid fund to help those who could not afford to bring their cases before the military courts and hundreds were submitted.

One of the first recipients of legal aid from the Al Haq fund was the farmer Sabri Gharib, who lived in the village of Beit Ijza, south of Ramallah. He was known to us because his was the very first sworn affidavit Al Haq obtained in 1982. In it he had testified about the relentless harassment by the settlers of Givon Ha'hadasha, which was being established next to his land. This included preventing him from cultivating his land, shooting at him and his children, threats to demolish his home and repeated night arrests by the Israeli military.

Sabri and his family stood their ground. Their ordeal lasted for over twenty-four years. It was still continuing when I visited him in May 2006. Despite the incessant pressure he had managed to stay in his house at the top of the hill. But now the settlement surrounded the house from three sides. A wire fence was built around the house leaving him a passageway only a few metres wide. He was only able to save a fraction of his agricultural land; the rest was taken over by the settlement. The current issue that was absorbing his attention when I visited was that the Separation Wall Israel was building would cut him off from his village and the houses he had built for his children down the hill. He would end up on the side of the settlement, an unwelcome Gentile in the midst of housing planned only for Jews. As he had done since 1982 in the course of his relentless attempts to save his land, he was now contesting the path of the wall at the Israeli High Court of Justice, adding another case to the numerous earlier challenges he took to that court expecting justice, only to be rebuffed time and time again. Sabri and I were standing outside in the sun looking at the settlement through the wire fence built around his house. He was telling me about this latest case when we saw an old man walking his Labrador on the other side of the fence. I tried hard to catch the man's eye. I wanted some indication of how he felt confining his neighbour in this way, but the man would not raise his eyes from the ground. He went solemnly through his walk, keeping pace with his dog, never showing any recognition of Sabri or his guest.

The resilience and courage of this man were legendary. But the long gruelling struggle against the settlers, the World Zionist Organization and the military government supporting them was taking its toll on Sabri, whose name means patience. His health was deteriorating though he still had fire in his big black fearless eyes as he spoke with courage and confidence about his plight. It was only on my last visit that I discovered that Sabri, who had ten children, was an only child. He had inherited from his father the large area of family land which he was deter-mined to preserve and pass on to his children. I also realized that the courageous fighter was not concerned with nationalist issues. He believed only in two constants, God and the land. Not to fight in every way possible to hold on to his land was sacrilege.

In those early days of our legal struggle before the big settlement thrust that began in the early eighties, Jonathan and I could fantasize how we were going to save the hills of Palestine from Jewish settlements. We were both dreamers, confident that we had the energy and the determination to make our plan work. We were challenging the very basis of the Israeli government's land acquisition policy. We also wanted to exhaust the military court system and hoped to delay the settlements until the cases had been heard. Now some twenty-five years later those times seem aeons away. How complicated and dismal the future has turned out, with the land now settled by close to half a million Israeli Jews, living in hundreds of settlements scattered throughout our hills and connected by wide roads crossing through the wadis. And more recently a wall has looped around the 'settlement blocs', destroying the beauty of our hills, separating our villages and towns from each other and annexing yet more of our land to Israel, demolishing the prospect for a viable peace.

Alone and without Jonathan I did not stop for long on the rock that marked the halfway point of the walk. I continued down the valley, which had now narrowed and was called Wadi El Kalb ('the dog'), where the water would tumble during the heavy rains. But I did not walk down that narrow wadi. I stayed to the left of it, following a path which was green and meandering, a happy path with rocks to step on to avoid squashing the young grass and delicate crocuses that lay between.

I continued on this path for some ten minutes until I got to A'yn El Asfourah ('the bird') on the left-hand side of the wadi. To cross to it I had to walk over wide rocks which were mossy, wet and slippery. Next to them and close to the ground was a cobweb of the green delicate leaves and yellow buds of chamomile. In the shallow ponds I could see tadpoles wriggling through the water. There was a drop down to a lower level of the valley, where in heavy rain waterfalls developed. Here the path forked. It continued southward up the hill called Jabal El 'qda, behind which was the village of A'yn Arik, famous for its sweet spring water and pomegranate trees.

I took the path that continued down Wadi El Kalb to A'yn Qenya. Here it was narrow and overgrown with shrubs. I walked alongside the wadi, hopping over rocks that had been smoothed by the water washing over them in winter. I calculated that it would take me two days to walk to the coastal plain from here.

What would it have felt like if all the refugees of Lydda and Ramle who were forced out of their towns that hot July day in 1948 were to have walked through these hills and valleys back to their cities? Israel would not have allowed them to stay, but perhaps the symbolic return would have helped relieve the inherited horror of that exodus and the disgrace of being forced out of one's home. It would have been a symbolic return journey, a reverse exodus to wash away the shame of that first forced expulsion. Perhaps after it the two sides could have negotiated the other aspects of the problem. It was good to dream of this even when I knew it could not possibly happen. It was not uncommon for me to think of crazy schemes walking in these hills.

Where the old narrow road from Ramallah to A'yn

Qenya approaches the path in the valley I came upon cliffs which it was not possible to clamber over. They stood in a cluster like a gate blocking the wadi. The rocks from the east where I approached were packed closely together in an overhang, forming a sort of canopy below which one could take shelter from the rain and sun. I circled around these cliffs, joined the valley on the other side and continued my walk through Wadi El Kalb towards the A'yn Qenya spring which has given the village its name.

A'yn Qenya was a small village of fewer than a thousand inhabitants where the houses did not have running water. Every morning the women and children took their buckets and walked to the spring to fill up with water. Someone had a donkey which could transport two buckets at a time, balancing them on each side of its belly, then trotting slowly uphill over the stony path to make the delivery. When it was not on duty the donkey could be seen tethered by the road in the centre of the village. Recently it had given birth to a lovely young donkey, who stood quietly next to his mother, his head bent down, looking as happy as only a donkey can.

I can still remember the very first walk I ever took down to this village, when we spent the night sleeping on the very rocks on which I now stood. It was the summer of 1969. I was participating in the Ramallah Boy Scouts' work camp, the only time in my life I ever did. One evening around midnight a group of us decided to walk down to A'yn Qenya. I don't know why, perhaps because that evening we had had to listen to the defeated arguments of the Israeli-appointed mayor of Ramallah who had been invited to address us. His sloping shoulders moved up and down when he chuckled over his own jokes, causing his arms to swing. No one else smiled or even agreed with any of the points he was making. Or perhaps we set off on our walk simply to prove that we could. We were at that age. None of us knew the way.

Israeli soldiers had come through these same hills as conquerors two years earlier. Perhaps we thought we would be re-conquering the territory by overcoming our fear of the dark abyss. There certainly was something liberating about the adventure. The night was still. There was no moon to light our way. We were eight young and uncertain men in the dark and for the first time I understood how it was possible to feel comfort in numbers. The thumping of our boots was heavy and persistent. It came as a warning to all other creatures inhabiting these hills to move away, stay clear of our path if they did not wish to be crushed. One of us, Jad, cut a branch from an old tree and held it in front of him menacingly. None of us would admit fear. There was no question of stopping. After scrambling in the hills for a few hours we were exhausted. We had lost our way. We sprawled on some large slabs of rock and immediately succumbed to a deep slumber. It was not a prudent thing to do but we were young and adventurous. We only woke up with the sun and the sounds of morning: the braying of donkeys, the bleating of the sheep and the distant shouts of the women calling on their children to fetch water from the spring. Despite the pain in my neck and the back of my head from using a rock as a pillow, I still remember how I was carried away by those crystal-clear village sounds reverberating across the valley. I remember wondering whether people in the village were as fond as I was of this morning chorus. Was this why they spoke so loudly to each other? Or was the reason more practical, simply a way of communicating across the hills between houses scattered on either side, using the human voice to make up for the absence of telephones?

And then there was the enticing smell of *taboon*, bread that the villagers baked themselves on hot stones. It was cold and humid in the early hours of the morning and we were hungry. We followed the smell through the village and the women who were doing the baking generously offered us some loaves.

It was early on in the Israeli occupation. There was so much we still had to learn. Unlike the Gaza Strip, there was little armed resistance in the West Bank. The suffering was more subtle, from having to endure the shame of defeat. I was sixteen and wanted to express my full potential and strength. I was a romantic, striving for some sort of heroic role. I could not accept the mayor with his shaking shoulders, who advised us to be sensible and give up any thought of resisting, but neither did I know of a viable course of struggle. I was shackled by the prevailing fear and insecurity. I was on my way to university and was not sure how my life would turn out. My only certainty was that it was going to be here in Palestine. I was already resolute that I would never run away. Now, over a decade later, still a romantic, but not a hero, I arrived at the spring when the sun was still shining.

Stretching beyond, on the western hill, were the orchards and cultivated fields. The water of the spring collected in a pool which was used to irrigate the fields. Above this green section of the hill there were a number of stone houses, all deserted. They were surrounded by enormous oaks and pines. They had terraces with gorgeous views of the hills. No one had lived in these houses since the occupation. I could not see a road connecting them to the village, they could only be reached on foot, or by donkey or mule.

The sun was moving behind the hill to my left and I walked through the village in partial shade. I thought I would walk up the forested hill that bordered the village in the north and then turn back. As I approached, a herd of grey gazelles leaped ahead of me, making their way to the top in no time.

Perhaps it was the gazelles in flight that gave me the idea. I found myself wanting to race the sun so as to catch its last rays at the summit of the hill before it disappeared. I was not sure how much time I had but whatever it was I was determined to make my rendez-vous as a finale to this gorgeous day. I took off my jacket and shirt and ran up, naked to the waist. I was enjoying the bite of the cold wind on my bare skin. I had to twist and turn to avoid the numerous stones on the path. I felt like a horse placing its hoofs carefully to avoid spraining its ankle. I did not pause even when I was short of breath. I was determined to see the sun setting over the sea of Jaffa.

I made it. I got there just in time, panting heavily. The air was dry and fresh. Lower hills spread below me like a crumpled sheet of blue velvet with the hamlets huddled in its folds. There was Janiya, Deir Ammar and on the highest hill the attractive village of Ras Karkar, all spread below me. The further the hills the smaller they looked. The most distant was dark blue, like a little pond. One hill interlocked with another in a slow, gentle slope down to the coastal plain and ultimately the sea. I was standing on the highest hill before the drop. It felt as though I was by the edge of that table plateau in the centre of the West Bank of which Beit 'Ur and Albina's land constituted just another corner. I continued to take in the view as the last rays of the sun were making their final slow journey dropping gently into the horizon, which I could barely make out in the haze. I tried to hold my breath until the last sliver of the orange sun disappeared and all that was left was the pink light reflected by the clouds that scattered in the big sky all around me. At this moment the wind began to pick up as it always does after the sun has set.

I was unaware that this would be the last time I would be able to stand here on an empty hill. Shortly afterwards the Israeli authorities expropriated the land and used it to build the settlement of Dolev.

When I look back now at those years in the eighties when I could walk without restraint, I feel gratified to have used that freedom and taken all those walks and got to know the hills. There was one walk that I had always planned which to my great regret I never got round to taking. It would start from the west of Ramallah, through Beitunia to Wadi El Mahkwm, passing north of Beit 'Ur. In the course of preparing for the Albina case I had become familiar with that region west of Ramallah through the visits I made to my client's land. The path continues through the central hills, emerging in the coastal plain and on to the blue Mediterranean Sea. I had planned this walk so carefully. Now with the settlements and the Separation Wall it was impossible.

The Albina case had been one of the first land cases I handled. I had good evidence and high hopes that I would win it and manage to save the land and thwart the plans for building a settlement next to the village of Beit 'Ur. I can well remember how this case came to me.

I was in court for another case, one involving a

contract, when an old lean man, the salt of the earth, pulled me by the hand.

'You are François Albina's lawyer,' he asserted.

It was not a question. He had made his investigation and he was seeking me out.

'What of it?' I asked.

He then told me that the settlers had come for the land.

I can still hear the low bass voice of the old man tugging at my elbow: 'The settlers are moving in. You must do something about it.'

The old man was the *Mukhtar* (village elder) of Beit 'Ur El Fauqa (Upper Beit 'Ur because there is another village close by to the south which is called Beit 'Ur El Tahta). In the village, Albina was locally known as 'The Christian'. Next to the land of 'The Christian' was the land of 'The Jew'. The two plots were at the south-eastern border of the village, restricting its growth. During the Jordanian regime, the area owned by The Jew was placed under the Jordanian Custodian of Enemy Property (a governmental authority established by statute that protected land owned by Israeli Jews in the area that came under Jordanian rule after 1948), which fought valiantly to protect the land from trespassers. François Albina's father, Antoine, who had died a few years earlier, had bought the land in the early forties because he liked its location on top of one of the highest hills overlooking the coast. It might have attracted his attention on one of his drives up to Ramallah, where he lived, from Jaffa because it was right next to the road.

Further down from this land the Jordanian army had expropriated an area where they had established an army camp. But no one, neither private individuals nor officials, had encroached on Albina's land even though François was living in East Jerusalem, where he ran a travel agency. Private property was protected under Jordanian control. When the Israelis began to build their settlement the residents of the nearby village assumed that The Christian had sold his land to The Jew. But just in case this wasn't true, the *Mukhtar* after ascertaining that our office represented Albina, had come to court to tell me of the order for expropriating the land which the Israeli military custodian had served him in his capacity as the village elder.

I could tell by the sceptical manner in which the *Mukhtar* asked what we were going to do that he was probing for something. He wanted to know whether his suspicion that Albina had sold the land to Israeli Jews was well-founded and the order was just a camouflage to protect Albina and remove any suspicion of his treacherous act.

But Albina had not sold. He had often been told by his father about this land that had been bought during Mandate times, that it was a beautiful plot on a hill near Beit 'Ur El Fouqa, which overlooked the western plain and the sea. His father traded in real estate. He had bought many plots in different parts of the country for investment. No one had told Albina that the settlers were claiming it. It was only when I relayed the *Mukhtar*'s enquiry to him that he realized his land was endangered. Later, when I approached the Israeli Custodian who had signed the order served on the *Mukhtar* and presented him with the early registration documents pertaining to the land, he claimed that he didn't know that the land was privately owned. This was why he gave the order to the *Mukhtar*, he said. Of course, he could have consulted the land registry to which he had free access. Then he would have found out that there was registration, even if not final, in the name of Albina. Clearly he was not acting in good faith.

Now François Albina was a big man, portly, and difficult to miss. He smoked a pipe, wore overalls and was a jovial fellow with a large head. When I reported to him what the Custodian had told me he collapsed with laughter, showing his tobacco-stained teeth: 'I with my excessive weight of 92 kilograms an absentee? Am I that easy to miss?' Not only was he a big man but his travel agency had a large sign posted prominently on the side of the building right in the centre of Salah Ed Din Street, the main commercial road in East Jerusalem, declaring 'Albina Tours' in big bold black letters.

Still, the case was not as simple as I at first thought. In the course of it we had to go through the whole gamut of allegations used by the government to appropriate Palestinian lands.

The first claim put forward by the Custodian, that François was an absentee, was easy to defeat simply because he has been a resident of East Jerusalem all his life, living and working there. He was not one of those who left the country or had been thrown out during the 1967 war or since.

Then came the second preposterous claim. The Custodian of Absentee Properties, who also happened to be the Custodian of Government Land, now said that if François was not an absentee then his land must be public. 'But it isn't,' I said. 'It is registered in my client's name and I have documents to prove it.' I presented maps and early Ottoman and British registration certificates. But the Custodian claimed the maps did not tally with the land and the area to which the deeds pertained was not the same area that was the subject of the order. We went on with this until I believe I satisfied the court that the land was indeed privately owned.

There now came a third claim, that in the event the land was not owned by an absentee and was not public land it had been expropriated by the Jordanian government for military purposes. 'If this is so,' I said, 'then show me the expropriation order.' I brought the Jordanian Official Gazette to the court to prove that in every case when the Jordanian army expropriated land they published a corresponding order. This was what Jordanian law required and, indeed, the Jordanian army camp nearby was the subject of a published order. 'No need for an order,' responded the Custodian, 'the Jordanian army used the land and this proves the government had taken it.' 'What would they use it for?' I asked. 'You shall see,' he answered enigmatically and asked that the court make a site visit. A visit to the site by the entire court was duly scheduled.

For the first month on the case I had liaised only with the Custodian, who was sheepish and confused. I was hoping to get him to cancel the order. When we reached a deadlock, he advised me not to bother with the court, suggesting to me through gestures and winks that the land had already been taken and would never be returned. But of course I was not going to take this as an answer. I then had no choice but to put my trust, albeit reluctantly, in the due process of the court.

The president of this court, Abu El Afia, had been a student in the 1940s at the American University in Beirut, where I studied. Prior to 1948 he was a close friend of relatives of my partner and uncle, Fuad. He was now an established Israeli lawyer with expertise in land law. In fact both he and I had a common client in the British Consulate. He was their counsel for West Jerusalem; I represented them in the West Bank, including East Jerusalem. I believed I could depend on him to stop the legal distortions of the Custodian, who seemed determined to swindle this land.

By the time the case came to me, the Custodian had already leased the land. Work was being carried out laying the infrastructure of the settlement, as François discovered when he visited it. Almost all property designated for settlement is held by the Custodian of Government Land on behalf of the Israeli state. The Custodian then allocates the land through a long-term lease to the World Zionist Organization Settlement Division. The lease stipulates that the lessees may not sub-lease the land to a non-Jew. The Ministry of Defence must approve the allocation.

The work of establishing the new settlement on François's land was the responsibility of the Jewish Agency, the pre-state Zionist movement recognized by the British in the terms of their 1922 Mandate over Palestine which represented Palestine's Jews to the British Authorities, served the Jews as a government in the making and funnelled Jewish philanthropy from abroad to projects in Palestine. It is a sister organization of the World Zionist Organization, the international body created by Herzl in 1897 to promote Jewish nationalism. In 1948 the Agency turned over most of its functions to the new state but continued to exist as a conduit by which Diaspora Jews could keep up financial support, donating to a non-governmental organization rather than to a foreign state. A contract with the government had outlined a division of functions. It was considered a national institution along with the Jewish National Fund and its West Bank subsidiary Hamanuta, which bought and managed land holdings in the West Bank in the name of the Jewish people.

Before 1967 recommendations were made in Israel to reduce the Settlement Department. Building settlements to create facts, it was argued, belonged to the era of ethnic struggle, not to a time when a state existed. But the occupation of the Palestinian Territories in 1967 increased the appetite of the Israeli government for more land and this organization swelled rather than contracted.

I first asked for an injunction to stop the work on the land. 'Would I be willing to guarantee the losses of the other side?' the president of the committee wanted to know. 'Losses?' I asked. 'Whose losses?' 'The Jewish Agency's, of course. They have entered into contracts with big contractors,' said the president. 'If we stop them now from implementation, they would be liable to pay damages for breach of contract.' He would only be willing to grant the injunction, he said, if I was prepared to make a guarantee of a quarter of a million US dollars to compensate the organization for their losses in the event that there was a delay in carrying out the work already contracted. This refusal to grant the injunction did not bode well for the outcome. Work on the land continued as the court proceeded to hear the case. It was no longer only a matter between the confused Custodian and me. International organizations and large sums of American money had been mobilized to fight this battle.

I don't believe the president of the court was a proponent of the settlement project. He certainly was not a right-winger. Every Israeli Jew had to do his stint of reserve duty and this was an easy way of carrying it out. Nurit, the court secretary, would call his office and arrange the time and venue that suited him. On the designated day, he donned his army uniform and spent a few hours in service of the state without the inconvenience of going to barracks or tents out in the field. The site visit requested by the representative of the state was the only field trip he had to do and it was bearable enough. We were able to drive to the land.

But my worries about the integrity of the court were exacerbated when the president repeatedly called me to the bar. Sometimes his tone was that of: 'You Arabs are always hard-headed and are never willing to compromise, won't you prove to be an exception?' At other times he used the tone of an elder giving good sensible advice to a stubborn, foolhardy younger man. In both instances he was urging me to advise my client to sell his land, implying that it was lost anyway. He had tired eyes with bags below them. He ended with an edge of exasperation, saying: 'At least get your client some money.' But I wouldn't give in. My whole purpose was to save the country, not sell its land away to the enemy. Fortunately my client, to whom I felt duty-bound to relay all these messages, did not want to sell either. As I expected, he was no less a patriot than myself. I was relieved. Because of the abundance of evidence and near-final registration, this was the best possible case I could ever hope to get. I was determined to win it, to show before the whole world the lie of those settlers who were claiming that they were only taking land that did not belong to anyone.

I had heard and read much about the crazy settlers and their even crazier Rabbis, and on the day designated for the site visit was expecting a lively encounter with a group of very strange people.

The road we took to Beit 'Ur was still that narrow winding road from Mandate times which my parents used every year before 1948 to travel from Jaffa to their summer house in Ramallah, a mere hour and forty minutes' drive. It was that same road they took on that fateful day in 27 April 1948, when they left behind everything they owned, never to return except as wistful visitors. Since then we had been stuck behind these hills and confined, away from our chosen home in the cosmopolitan city by the coast. How utterly miserable it must have been for my father to have been forced to return to the land of Abu Ameen and the provincial life of Ramallah. But for me, it was the only life I knew.

In 1948 the Jewish forces lost many of their fighters trying to reach Jerusalem through the only corridor that stretched from the coast to the city. It has been the consistent policy of successive Israeli governments since 1967 to plant settlements around Jerusalem to ensure that the city could be reached through another access route, which would eventually be annexed to Israel, thickening the seam around the city's north-western border. The settlers, driven by religious motives, were convenient agents for the state to fulfil its strategic objectives. They had its full support.

The old Ramallah–Jaffa road, which we took when the court was making its site visit, was built when roads still followed the contours of the hills, long before the affluent Israeli government began digging deep into them, slicing them open to make roads that were straight and level and could quickly get settlers from the centre of the country to the Jewish suburbs, cutting the travelling time from Jaffa to Tel Aviv by half. This was an important development and selling point that convinced many

Israelis to live in these areas on the West Bank. This old road climbed up the highest hill, passing close to Albina's land. François's father might have walked up and been dazzled by the gorgeous view overlooking the Mediterranean and the clean fresh air. Perhaps he thought that one day he would build himself a summer house there.

It took a little over twenty minutes to reach the land from Ramallah. Just before we got to it we passed the Jordanian army camp to the right of the road. This land had already been taken over by the settlers, who had placed ugly red-coloured caravan-style houses on it. Then came the empty plot owned by 'The Jew'. The original owner of this land was from the village. It is said by people there that he was forced to sell it before 1948 to raise money to pay the defence lawyer handling the case of his son, who was accused of murder during the British Mandate. After 1967, rather than return Jewish absentee properties to their individual owners, Israel reclaimed them in the name of the Jewish people out of fear that if it gave them back to individual Israeli Jews, Palestinian absentees who owned land in Israel would request similar treatment. The existence of this plot must have alerted the Custodian to my client's land. He now had a peg on which to hang his claim, starting from a small plot and ending up grabbing the whole hill. Albina's land stretched along the side of the hill, reaching all the way up to the first houses in the village. The settlers had connected the first plot with Albina's by an unpaved road.

The wind was very strong that day. We had to battle against it on our way up the hill from the temporary structures, using the dirt road dug by the settlers. An American settler enthusiastically pointed to clefts in the ground which he said were trenches that the Jordanian army had built, evidence, as he explained, that this was not private but state land which Israel was now entitled to take back. The judges remained impassive. Like me, the president knew very well that Jordanian law required that an expropriation order be issued. We had already been through this. After struggling with the wind and the hill we were cold and tired. We were all invited to have tea in the community hall of the fledgling settlement.

At the settlement headquarters I was expecting to meet devils incarnate, fanatic, crazy people, starry-eyed and religiously inspired, who were forcing us to a confrontation and to many years of bloodshed. The prospect of coming face to face with these settlers filled me with a sense of excitement and adventure. I wondered how these evil people would look and act. How would they behave towards me? Would I be safe in their midst?

We were met by earnest-looking men, with no women. They served us tea in Styrofoam cups. We sat around a long table. I felt myself a witness to what it must have been like for the old Zionist settlers. I expect their latterday counterparts were living out an old dream. They were in their thirties and were wearing jeans. Many were bearded. They seemed amiable. They were not starry-eyed, they were hard-headed men who were fully committed to what they were doing and had no conception of how Albina, the victim of their actions, would see them. Nor did they seem to care. I doubt, if I had articulated to them my deeply held convictions and arguments against the settlement project, that they would have even heard me, so full were they of their own sense of purpose.

Their enthusiasm was contagious. Had I not been on the other side, I could have fallen for it. They were literally camping on the land, pushing out their enemies and expanding the area of their state, perhaps carried away by a *sarha* of their own. What were a few legal objections against the elevated nobility of their purpose? They had none of the looks or mannerisms I attributed to evil people.

Nor were they crazy. They were efficient and calculating businessmen who wanted to get over this legal hurdle. What surprised me even more was the lack of guilt they exhibited towards me. I was the representative of the owner of the land whose property they were taking, or, more accurately, stealing. I had expected they would at least be apologetic or timid in my presence. They were not. They cared little about the Palestinians in Beit 'Ur, who had been in the village for centuries and were now going to be edged out by the new settlement which these men were establishing from their office hardly five hundred metres away. Nor did they have any qualms, as I discovered later, about using any sort of trickery or deceit to get their way. To them the end seemed to justify the use of any means. This was how those who believed they were serving a higher purpose behaved.

The settlement to be established on the land was given the name Bet Horon, Horon being the Canaanite deity mentioned in Ugaritic literature. Biblical tradition attributes the founding of both Lower and Upper Beth-Horon to Sheerah, daughter of Beriah, son of Ephraim (I Chronicles 7:24). With the exception of this ancient biblical link, the settlement being planned on my client's land had nothing to do with religious Zionism. It was planned to attract ordinary middle-class, secular Israelis, not believers, who wanted to live in the quiet of the countryside with breathtaking views and a commute to Tel Aviv of less than an hour.

When Jonathan and I sat on that rock and plotted how we were going to frustrate the whole of the settlement project through legal action we did not know that the legal aspects were only one small, ultimately insignificant, component. The building of settlements in the Occupied Territories was a state project. It was not going to be hampered by questions of law. The custodians, legal advisors and judges would have to work out amongst themselves the legal solutions. The government knew the decision it wanted out of these land courts. Higher national objectives overrode legal niceties.

I remember well that last session in the case when, having attempted many other tricks, the Custodian tried to prove to the court that the land was used by the Jordanian army by bringing an Arab youth to testify. The weather had worsened and the courthouse was getting darker. Outside it was cold and misty. There was a rumour that it was going to snow. We were ensconced in the over-heated Russian Compound, the *Mascobieh,* that housed the Israeli court, a police station and a prison where several Palestinians have lost their lives under torture. The president of this tribunal, Abu El Afia, an Israeli Jew with an Arabic surname that means the father of vitality, had frog eyes that opened wide as he attempted to infuse these sham proceedings with a veneer of respectability. His two colleagues on the bench were mostly silent. On his right was a chocolate factory owner, a young handsome man who looked totally distracted, perhaps thinking of his chocolates. The third judge was a meek-looking man, probably a government official in disguise.

A young Arab man was brought in by the state attorney and presented as a witness. His head was wrapped entirely in a black and white *kuffieh,* the chequered headscarf favoured by older Palestinians, leaving only slits for the eyes. He was to testify that he had trained with the Jordanian army right there on that wretched land of Albina's. I objected strongly to this witness. He must show his face, I insisted, there was no reason to bring him to the stand disguised in this manner. Dani Kramer, the state representative, was not prepared to give me the witness's name or age. Clearly he looked too young to have served in the Jordanian army fifteen years ago. I said all this to the panel of judges. The president seemed embarrassed. He knew that this was not right. There was no justification for disguising the identity of a witness in a civil case.

At this point Dani Kramer went forward to the podium and whispered something to the court president that I couldn't hear. He promptly agreed that the masked man could testify with his head covered. The man with the piercing eyes and covered head proceeded to recite everything he had been drilled to say. I suspected that he might have been paid for this either with money or more likely in kind, in the form of a grant of permits from the military authorities which he or members of his family needed.

Who, I wondered, was behind the mask? I thought I recognized those eyes. They looked fervently at me as though they wanted to communicate something. What was it? An apology or a plea to understand and condone? They were not mean or vindictive. They were anxious. What sort of man would accept to testify, lie like this, betray his country?

And there I was with my colleague, Mona Rishmawi, anxious, tense, the two of us trying to do our best, wondering whether we should go on with this farce.

Was it good for Palestine for us to continue to the end or were we only lending legitimacy to an illegal court? The state attorney and the panel of judges were discussing amongst themselves, constantly consulting. There was no one else in that courtroom that day.

I looked out of the window; the clouds were gathering. The weather was worsening. The witness was completing his testimony. It was all so dark and tragic and in such contrast with the purity of the reluctant snow that had started falling. Soon it would cover the red-tiled roof of the *Mascobieh*. The attractive building with a courtyard in the middle would be transformed by a soft white cover. Even the barbed wire over the wall would lose its sting. If the snow should settle on the roads, I would have a hard time getting back to Ramallah. My car was not equipped for such conditions and I was not a good driver under the best of circumstances.

We went through the charade. The masked young man testified that he had taken part in the civil defense unit of the Jordanian army and that they did their training on the hill in question and that they had used these trenches on Albina's land. 'So what?' I argued. 'What did this prove? What if the army had dug trenches? They could do this and still the land would remain private. The land doesn't miraculously get transformed the moment the army touches it. It only changes hands when it is expropriated and this never happened.' Like me the president knew this all too well but would he have the professional integrity and courage to rule in accordance with the law?

I looked up again at the long window. The snow continued to fall, hesitant, cottony. As I sat listening to the drone of Dani Kramer, I was getting distracted by the downy flakes waltzing to the pavement outside, covering the dirt and squalor. I could hardly wait for that day's session to end. When I left I would see a transformed world. Even the notorious prison house next to the court would be covered in pure white. I began to fret again about getting back.

We managed to get out of Jerusalem and back to Ramallah without difficulty, but once there found that the snow was deeper than in Jerusalem. Driving up a side road to the main road I decided not to stop at the stop sign, afraid that the car might skid. At that moment, an Israeli army jeep happened to pass by. It swerved and drew up right next to me. Why did I not stop, the soldiers asked. They found my behaviour suspicious. I tried to explain but they were not convinced. They assumed I was running away from them. It was only the intervention of a taxi driver who recognized me and put in a good word with the soldiers, with whom he seemed to be suspiciously friendly, that they let me go. I was saved from arrest on that cold snowy day by the intervention of a probable collaborator.

A few months after that walk to A'yn Qenya, the decision in the Albina case was handed down. No session was held for reading the decision, it was mailed to me. The Military Objections Committee found that 'There is no doubt in our eyes that the appellant (Albina) is the legal owner of the land in question.' Even so, the Committee decided that the transaction which the Custodian had made with the Zionist Agency to lease the land for a period of forty-nine years 'is in fact standard, strong and binding and this in spite of the fact that we concluded in our opinion that the ownership of the said land belongs to the appellant'. They based this strange decision on Article 5 of Military Order 58, which states that 'Any transaction carried out in good faith between the Custodian of Absentee Property and any other person, concerning property which the Custodian believed when he entered into the transaction to be abandoned property, will not be void and will continue to be valid even if it were proved that the property was not at that time abandoned property.'

In my summing up I had anticipated the possibility that they might invoke this article and had written: 'If Article 5 is not interpreted strictly and the Custodian then believes that whatever action he takes (even if based on improper legal considerations) would be retroactively validated by imputing to it good faith, without using strict criteria to ascertain whether or not it in fact existed, the Custodian would in effect be given a free hand to act arbitrarily ... If this happens, a mockery would have been made of the law.'

This statement seems to have had no effect on the court. Not only had the court found a way to justify the takeover of my client's land – it did not even order that my client be paid any compensation. Abu El Afia proved his worth as a loyal Israeli. I was only glad that I had not recommended that my client put up the quarter-of-a-million-dollar guarantee requested by the court as a condition for granting the injunction to stop work on the land pending completion of the case.

According to the Jordanian land law that continued to be in force in the West Bank, long-term leases in land must be registered at the Land Registration Department having jurisdiction over the land. I asked Ghazi, the Land Registrar, whether the lease over Albina's land was registered at the Ramallah Registry, whose jurisdiction included Beit 'Ur. He said it wasn't. Where then was this lease registered? I had once come upon a military order which enigmatically referred to 'Special Transactions in Land' that would be registered in a 'Special Land Registration Department'. I had always assumed that since this register was not at the Ramallah Land Registration Department it must be located at the Headquarters of the Military Commander of the West Bank in Beit El, not in Israel, since the land was in the Occupied Territories. Years later I happened to be checking on a plot of land for a client in Jerusalem and discovered that land leases involving Jewish settlements in the occupied West Bank were registered at the Israel Land Authority, where all Israeli state land is registered. With this discovery the last piece of the puzzle fell into place. I realized that to all intents and purposes the lands on which West Bank Jewish settlements were established are considered by Israel as Israeli land. The ideological position that the West Bank belonged by divine edict to Israel was given full force in secular legal terms and through elaborate administrative arrangements that ensured that the land was annexed to Israel in every aspect except by name.

On 15 November 2006, a holiday commemorating Palestine's Independence Day, I went to Beit 'Ur to visit the writer Adel Samara. I also wanted to see what had become of the Albina land. It was no longer possible to get to the village using the short direct route, which would have taken twenty minutes. Instead I had to travel west then south then east again, in a big loop, through the villages of A'yn Arik, Deir Ibzi, Kafr Ni'ma, Safa, Beit 'Ur El Tahta and finally after a ninety-minute tortuous trek over narrow winding roads through the hills and valleys to Beit 'Ur El Fauqa. Once in the village I could hear the hum of the heavy traffic on Route 443 that replaced the old road which had once connected Beit 'Ur and Ramallah to the coastal plain, passing through the centre of the village. The new road, built south of the old one, bypassed the village. Even though the new road included a 9.5 kilometre stretch in the West Bank and was built on lands appropriated from six Palestinian villages for 'public needs', including the agricultural lands of Beit 'Ur, the Israeli army prohibited Palestinians from using it and had closed the exit to Beit 'Ur with cement blocks. Adel, who lived in the village and had to commute daily to Ramallah, where he worked, pointed to the road which we could see below and said: 'Look at this graphic example of discrimination.' He told me that his family owned olive groves on the other side of the road but could not pick the olives because of the danger of crossing a busy highway without a pedestrian crossing.

To get to Adel's house in the centre of the small village of 800 inhabitants we drove over the same segments of the old road that I had driven on when I visited with the court. I remembered the store where we used to stop to buy home-baked *taboon* bread. It was still there, but today I had no stomach for food.

I drove up to Albina's land, climbing up to the highest point in the village and passing by the half-demolished ancient Ottoman fortification. Adel pointed out the hole in the tower caused by the shelling of the Ottoman garrison protecting the road north of Jerusalem in the First World War from the force commanded by General Sir Edmund Allenby stationed on the opposite hill to the east of the village. After a short drive down the slope we came upon a five-metre wall, made of concrete and steel, that enclosed the entire Albina land. I gasped when I saw it. I remembered the gentle slope bordered by a few pine trees. Now there was a rude termination of the ancient village as though a prison had been placed at the southern tip of the hill. The wall enclosed an estate of expensive villas housing wealthy Israelis, mainly technicians working in information technology. They had their backs turned to their Palestinian neighbours, making the point in as blunt and rude a manner that they belonged to another world, that of a modern consumer society which subsidizes luxury homes built on land that came to it free of charge, with breathtaking views and clean air, connected to the centre of the country by a fast four-lane highway built on their neighbours' land and to which their neighbours had no access. No part of the settlers' dwellings, not even the roofs of their villas, could be seen from the village, only the high street lights that were lit all day and night to provide further protection in case one of the village youths decided to put a ladder up and climb the wall and attack the settlement. I had intended to inquire from Adel about relations between the inhabitants of the settlement and the village, who seemed of almost equal numbers. But when I saw how things looked on the ground there was no point in asking. The answer was writ large in the most graphic way possible.

Standing before the wall I could see in concrete terms the consequence of the policy of building Jewish settlements pursued by successive Israeli governments over the past thirty-nine years. For an occupier to take through legal chicanery the lands of the occupied, and in stark violation of international law settle its own people in the midst of the towns and villages of the hostile occupied population, can only lead to violence and bloodshed. There is no way that such usurpation of land could be accepted. A bloody struggle was inevitable. A high wall dividing the mixed population living on the same hill in Beit 'Ur and Bet Horon will not placate anyone. It only shields the usurpers from the anger and hatred in the eyes of those whose village has been unjustly divided, whose life and movement have been restricted, whose future has been doomed.

The mighty wall stretched from the top of the hill down to the road, leaving outside its borders the southern slope, where some villagers had their homes. The government school serving several villages, including the two Beit 'Urs, stood at the bottom of the hill – sandwiched between the wall and the new highway. The school and houses were reached by a steep, narrow, asphalted road bordering the wall. We could see some twelve-year-old boys returning from school, carrying their heavy bags up the hill. Adel pointed out that twice a day they pass along this ugly, prohibitive structure when in the past they had a panoramic view of the entire valley to the east. 'What will they grow up thinking?' he wondered aloud.

I parked the car and we stood at the top of the hill, where the wall looped, looking at the hills and Wadi Jaryout to the north. A military road, another one dug by the Israeli army through the hills, had recently been opened, connecting Bet Horon to Jerusalem and skirting the town of Beitunia south of Ramallah from the east. Adel explained that this road would border the wall that was to be constructed, expropriating the entire hill north of the village and connecting with the wall around Bet Horon. This would place the settlement within one of the 'settlement blocs' north of Jerusalem that Israel planned to annex. I asked Adel whether the area we were looking at had good walking tracks. He told me that when he was young he often walked from his village to Ramallah through Wadi Jaryout and remembered the track very well. He also told me that there were two *Maqamat* (shrines for holy men) along the way; one was called Maqam Abu Żaitoun and the other Maqam Um El Sheikh, who he presumed was the mother of the first saint. Along the way were two springs: the one that was fastest flowing with the sweeter water remained active throughout the year was called A'yn Jaryout. The other was A'yn Meita.

'And what about this valley that we can see going to the west?' I asked.

'This is a wide beautiful valley we call Wadi El Mallaqi ('the wadi of meetings'). Perhaps it was given this name because it connected many villages from the central hills and the coastal plain.'

I realized this was the wadi I had long wanted to take to fulfil my ambition of walking from the Ramallah hills to the coastal plain and the sea. Now it was too late. Even if I risked scrambling the heights of Beit 'Ur to get down to the wadi I would hardly be able to walk a fifth of the way. Once by the village of Bil'in to the north-west I would meet with the newly constructed wall, and even if I should manage to cross it the numerous Moodi'n settlements built in the wadis and over the hills along with the other settlements that straddle the green line would block my way. This is one walk I will never be able to take.

❧

I will always associate the path down the A'yn Qenya valley with my bachelor days. Six years later, when Penny and I were married at the height of the Palestinian Intifada in 1988 and, a few days after the Palestinian declaration of independence, we moved to a new house further down the road from my old place. We began to take walks in Wadi El Wrda, the Abu Ameen wadi, just behind where we lived. But then one afternoon, in the summer of 1999, Penny called me at the office.

'How about a walk in the hills?' she asked.

I was ready to leave the office and welcomed the suggestion. She had in mind, she said, a walk in the A'yn Qenya valley which we had long neglected.

We were well into the Interim Phase, the five-year period designated by the Oslo Accords before negotiations would begin for determining the final status of the Occupied Territories. It was then that the fate of the settlements was to be decided. The Palestinian hope for a better future and an end to the conflict was reflected in the higher levels of investment, much of it going into construction. Ramallah was already hemmed in from the east and south by Jewish settlements. The only land left for the town to expand into was the hills to the north and west, which were quickly being developed by new Palestinian construction. Not far from our house Birzeit University was completing a housing development for its employees. A new private school had also been constructed, as well as a number of attractive villas, signalling new wealth for the emerging elites. As a result of all this we had to walk further up the road before we could begin our descent into the valley. But everywhere we went we found piles of rubble that had been dumped down the side of the hill. We first tried going down one but the dirt was too soft and slippery to trudge over and we couldn't make it. We continued through the building site until we found a spot where I thought we could descend since it had a makeshift path created by concrete which must have been poured there by mistake. We made it down and I suggested to Penny that we first visit the nearby *qasr*. From there we began our descent, risking the possibility that we might have to walk back in the dark.

It was then that we heard shots. I thought they were close, but ever optimistic, Penny thought we were only hearing echoes. More shots followed, louder and closer. They could not be echoes. One whizzed overhead, and Penny fell to the ground. I feared she had been shot.

She hadn't. She lifted her head and said: 'I think we're being shot at.'

I held her hand and we ran to take shelter against a rock that formed the wall of one of the terraces down the side of the hill. The shots were coming from behind us, from above. We hoped that by flattening our bodies against the rock no part of us would be exposed to the fire.

I could not understand what was happening. Who was shooting and were we the target or did we just happen to be in the way?

I looked around me to see if something else was going on further down the hill, but could not see or hear anything. The shooting intensified. I decided we *must* be the target. But why?

Since the PLO took over in Ramallah the Israeli army had not been venturing into the town. It was unlikely that those shooting at us were Israeli soldiers. But then why would the Palestinian police shoot at us? Could it be because they took us for settlers? If so, I could correct this mistaken impression.

I raised my hat and waved it, shouting as loud as I could, in Arabic: 'Why are you shooting at us? Stop shooting, for God's sake, stop, stop.' But either my hat was not impressive enough, or my voice did not carry, or perhaps they just did not care either way, for the shooting continued.

'They can't think we're settlers,' Penny gasped. 'They wouldn't shoot at Jews. It's too complicated. So stop endangering your life.'

The shooting continued mercilessly, giving us no respite, no time to take a breath, to think calmly of our next step, to manage, somehow, to escape. A hail of bullets whizzed overhead, struck the rock right in front of where we took shelter, sending splinters up in the air. It seemed likely that some of the bullets would ricochet and hit us.

When finally there was a brief lull I tried again. This time I stepped forward. Perhaps showing my person would be more impressive than waving my hat. I turned and looked up. I could see them. Two young Palestinian men in jeans standing on top of one of the unfinished buildings brandishing their guns at me. They could see me, I was sure of it. I thought that now they had seen me they would stop. But they didn't. I threw myself back at the rock just in time as the young men showered us with more bullets. I now became convinced they were not going to stop until they got us. As I crouched behind that rock I was not sure things had really improved since the days when Israel's direct rule had ended. Our ordeal lasted for twenty long minutes.

After the guns fell silent, we waited another five minutes before we slid away on wobbly knees, heads bent, keeping close to the rocks on the terrace wall, tired, distracted and despondent. When we got to the road, we walked down towards the Palestinian checkpoint at the end of Tireh road, not far from where we were almost killed. We wanted to report what had happened to the soldiers there. The first young man in fatigues we met had the decency to listen. He could see how shaken we were. He confirmed that he knew there were two young men shooting in the hills. He must have heard them. But then his older and more senior colleague joined him and asked what the matter was. The younger Palestinian began to recount our story but the senior official did not want to listen. He made a gesture with his hand to silence him. He sent us away, refusing to speak to us or hear our report.

For days after this incident Penny kept telling me that I should tell the *Muhafiz* (the Palestinian Governor) what had happened, that I should lodge a formal written complaint. I considered the matter very carefully. For most of my working life I had been urging people to use the law to submit legal complaints. But now I was reluctant to take any form of legal action. From my knowledge of the Oslo Accords and the local law I was fully aware that there was a failure to delineate the distinction between criminal action punishable by the law and legitimate action taken in resistance to the occupation. This blurring of the margins meant confusion and a legal vacuum that made it impossible to know under which law the action of these young men would be punishable or to whom one should direct one's criminal complaint. Nor could I find a law that established and regulated the functioning of the armed forces on which I could base my complaint. With so many unknowns how could I draft the complaint? Then one day the *Muhafiz*, who has known my family for many years, happened to come to our office to discuss a matter with my partner regarding a civil case in which he had an interest. I took the opportunity to tell him of what happened in the hills. After I finished he became visibly nervous.

'You shouldn't go to the valley,' he said. 'The *shabab* [young men] are always shooting there. That's where they practise. Just a few days ago they said we haven't shot for a while and went shooting.'

He called his *murafiq* (guard) and asked: 'When did you last go shooting?'

'Tuesday.'

He turned to me and said: 'You see. That's the day you told me the incident happened. Isn't it so?' He spoke again to his *murafiq*. 'Where did you go shooting?'

'Behind Tireh, near the Mustaqbal School.'

'You see. It's close to where you described.' He asked his *murafiq*, 'What time?'

'Eleven at night.'

'We were shot at much earlier,' I said. 'And we were not behind the school. We were further up. Not far from the checkpoint. They mustn't do this,' I said. 'There are shepherds there and others who walk in the hills. I have been walking for twenty-five years. Nothing ever happened to me in these hills. I never had to worry. People should be encouraged to walk in the hills. It will increase their attachment to their country.'

The *Muhafiz* didn't agree. 'You shouldn't walk,' he repeated in a concerned paternal tone. 'It's much too dangerous.'

'Perhaps your soldiers thought that I was going off for a fling with a foreign woman,' I suggested. 'And they wanted to spoil it for us. But really, I with my bald head and Penny with her greying hair. Not much of wild youth there.'

'*Khisarah ala Ramallah* ['Pity Ramallah'],' the *Muhafiz* said, standing up.

I don't know what he meant. Did he feel embarrassed that he was helpless to do anything? Did he feel sorry that I, the son of his friend, Aziz Shehadeh, who in his time was one of the most powerful men in the community, should be reduced to a situation where, when he's shot at in the hills, he can do nothing about it? I don't know, I never asked.

Another six years and another Intifada, and again I went down to that same valley. This time I was with a Palestinian-Dutch poet, Ramsey Nasr. I had met him at a poetry reading held at the Divan Coffee Shop in Ramallah and invited him for a walk in the hills. He was very excited because he liked fossils and hiking. We hired a taxi to take us to the narrow road that leads to the waste water purification plant behind Mustaqbal School. Then we walked down the narrow road.

It was about four in the afternoon. The day had become cloudy but it was not yet raining. New buildings and roads were quickly being built in the terraces below the Birzeit University Housing Development. I expected building would soon reach all the way down to the wadi. The altar rock with the dinosaur footprints did not have long to survive, I thought. Already many of the paths I had walked were covered by the rubble dumped down from the higher terraces. Eventually we managed to get beyond these mounds of loose dirt and rocks, found the path and began following it. We talked as we walked and got to know each other. Soon we arrived at the first large rock, which I remembered was close to my rock with the fossilized footprints. I looked for it but could not find it. Meanwhile I could hear dogs barking not far away from the appropriately called Wadi El Kalb ('the dog'). I wondered how many there were and whether they would attack us. I asked Ramsey to stay put as I criss-crossed the terraces looking for the rock. Then finally, much further down than I remembered, I found it. By now the barking dogs were getting closer. They were wild, in a pack, and might be rabid and dangerous. I cut some stems from dead *natsh* and carried them with me, thinking that if the dogs attacked I would have something to defend myself with, another important use to which *natsh* can be put.

At first Ramsey was not overly impressed with the rock. But then when I pointed out to him its different features he began to see how it could be the imprint of a dinosaur's foot. I wondered whether he would turn our adventure in the endangered Ramallah hills into a poem in Dutch. He wanted to take pictures. He was slow and took his time. The light was fading. Raindrops were beginning to fall and the dogs' barking was getting closer. I kept my ears tuned to the dogs, hoping we could leave before disaster struck. Ramsey was admiring another stone with root fossils. I offered it to him. He hesitated. 'Take it,' I said. He did and thanked me as if it belonged to me. He was very polite.

Finally he was done. He had taken all the pictures he needed and we started walking up. I was armed with my *natsh* and he carried his plastic bag holding an Arabic dictionary that he had bought that afternoon for his father and the rock with the fossilized roots. I hurried on ahead of him.

'Good host that you are,' I heard him call, 'would you

give me a branch if these dogs attacked?' He must have been as concerned about these dogs as I was.

'No,' I said jokingly. 'It's every man for himself in these hills.'

A short while later I heard him say in his soft voice: 'Look up! There are soldiers. They have guns.'

I had been too busy negotiating my way between the rocks to notice.

'Soldiers? What kind? Israeli or Palestinian?' I asked, somewhat breathlessly.

I looked up. There were men in fatigues silhouetted against the horizon a few terraces above, pointing their guns down at us. Whether Israeli or Palestinian, soldiers look out of place in these hills, as perhaps they do on any hill, anywhere in the world.

What could have brought Israeli soldiers into Ramallah? What did they think was happening here?

But when I looked more carefully I realized the men looked too passive to be Israeli soldiers. I greeted them in Arabic. At first they didn't respond. I decided to walk slowly towards them trying to remain as calm and composed as possible, suppressing my anger at their intrusion of our walk.

When I got to them, I told them who I was. They asked what I was doing.

'Walking,' I said. I didn't want to tell them more.

It was now raining hard.

'Can we see identification?'

I took out my wallet, which luckily I was carrying, pulled out my lawyer's card and showed it to them.

'What are you doing walking in this weather, at this time?' they asked, as though this was a place of extreme danger, the valley of the shadow of death.

'Walking,' I repeated. Then added: 'We went down to see a particular rock with dinosaur footprints.'

I thought the dinosaur might interest them. But they were not impressed.

'How did you know we were here?' I asked.

'It's our duty to protect our guests. We thought this foreigner was being kidnapped. We have surrounded the area. We have people on the other side of the valley as well.'

He pointed to the hills across from the valley up from A'yn Arik. They had clearly mounted a military operation to capture me and save Ramsey.

He radioed the other soldiers. 'It's OK,' he told them, speaking into his walkie-talkie.

I was still carrying the *natsh* I had picked up for protection from the barking dog 'I hope you didn't think this was a gun,' I said.

He dismissed the insinuation with a gesture of his hand. But he did say he suspected there were others down there with us, a whole troupe involved in the kidnap operation.

'I often come to walk in these hills,' I said to the man who was doing all the talking and seemed to be the commander. He was compact and short, not much taller than me, with dark black, intense eyes, and wearing soldier's fatigues. 'In fact I was once here with my wife, it was 1999, and some of your soldiers shot at us.'

'It was over on that side,' the soldier pointed out. 'I was there,' he said, smiling impishly.

'You could have killed us,' I said.

Another soldier added in a strange defence: 'The hills are dangerous, we have found many corpses here.'

As we all stood there in the dark, with the rain now

pouring heavily, I reflected on that dreadful afternoon six years ago. I never thought I'd ever meet one of the men who shot at Penny and me and almost killed us. He didn't seem particularly sorry, and certainly did not apologize though I was not expecting him to after all those years. Still I was grateful to be reminded that for every story there is an ending.

3

ILLUSORY PORTALS

Qomran, the Dead Sea and Wadi El Daraj

For many years I continued to contest acquisitions of Palestinian land for Jewish settlements before Israeli courts. As the Albina case had shown, even with the best of cases there could never be outright victories. What kept me going was the possibility of reducing the area of land which the often overzealous Custodian of Israeli Government and Absentee Properties claimed. I also believed that Israeli actions in taking Palestinian land should not go unchallenged. Successive Israeli governments continued to pursue a policy of settling the Occupied Territories. Billions of US dollars were spent on the project, money that sometimes had to be diverted from needy sectors in Israel itself. The Master Plan for the Central Region of the West Bank was followed with no less ambitious master plans for the north and the south. The government did all it could to implement them fully despite being in violation of international law.

Land acquisition was not the only prerequisite for settlement. Land use planning for their benefit was just as important. Its aim was to designate most empty land for their future use, isolate Palestinian population centres, and fragment their territorial continuity by encircling them with settlements. To achieve this, Regional Plans for the West Bank prepared during the British Mandate were altered and outline plans for most of the Palestinian towns and villages were prepared in great haste in the late eighties. These consisted of plans crudely drawn by felt-tip markers on photocopies of aerial photographs. Their main purpose was to determine the boundaries within which Palestinian urban development would be confined. Simultaneously outline plans for the Jewish settlements were being prepared with precisely the opposite objective. They reserved the maximum area of land for future development. Under the cloak of law, a highly discriminatory, segregated town-planning reality came into effect. It was to challenge the legality of these schemes that I applied myself during the last years of the 1980s.

The head of the Planning Council for the West Bank was an Israeli settler who was ideologically dedicated to the settlement project. Even when Palestinians found the financial resources to hire a town planner to prepare proper plans for their village, the Planning Council rejected them and held on to their crude drawings, which confined the village within a border drawn around existing construction. When I asked the head of planning how the village was expected to provide plots for the future expansion of its inhabitants, he would answer with a straight face that they could build up. The image of our beautiful villages in the undulating hills crammed with skyscrapers horrified me.

These developments were forcing me to rethink my strategies. Clearly the legal challenges were ineffective in curbing or even slowing down the extensive Jewish settlements. It was necessary to go beyond the framework of Israeli law and courts. When the Madrid International Peace Conference convened in September 1991 I welcomed the prospect of peaceful negotiations as the only possibility of regaining our usurped land.

But Israel had prepared well for what was coming. They succeeded in confining the scope of the negotiations to 'talks on interim self-government arrangements' for the Palestinians. The settlements, the land designated for them, and their administrative and legal links to Israel would be outside the scope of the conference. To enable the Palestinian delegation to argue convincingly the case for the inclusion of these issues was not going to be simple. The head of the Palestinian delegation asked me to help in devising a legal strategy to meet this challenge.

I studied the matter, made my proposals and travelled to Washington, where the negotiations were being held with great expectations. I soon discovered Yasser Arafat, the head of the PLO, instructing the delegation from Tunis, had different concerns. His main aim was to secure recognition for the PLO. Three years later, in the Declaration of Principles, this was achieved at the price of keeping the settlements out of the jurisdiction of the Palestinian Authority. This authority also had no power to change the village and town zoning schemes or repudiate Israeli claims over the land acquired for the settlements. I was dismayed and horrified. With one blow, political expediency led to the acceptance of all the illegal changes we in the Occupied Territories had been struggling to nullify for over two decades.

Yet despite their fundamental flaws, the Oslo Agreements were accepted by most Palestinians. When I expressed my oppositional view I was categorized as a rejectionist. To increase the popularity of the Accords, international funding flowed into the Occupied Territories aimed at distracting the population from continuing the struggle to end the occupation. Large grants became readily available for non-governmental organizations to carry out what was called democracy training, encouraging the illusion that Palestine had achieved self-determination and all that was lacking was for the population to be better schooled in democratic practices. With Israel still controlling the majority of the water resources, expensive programmes were introduced to teach people to conserve water. The huge capital infusion into the Occupied Territories meant that most people were willing to put aside the nationalist agenda which had dominated their lives for the previous quarter of a century. My eyes were opened to how fickle people can be and how it was possible to bring them to relinquish passionately held positions. The settlements which had been at the heart of our struggle against the occupation were all around us, Israel was continuing to expand them and establish new ones on our land, and yet people argued that the Oslo Accords provided the way for the future peace between us and the Israeli people.

Amongst the few concessions Israel was willing to make was to allow the return of a number of PLO cadres into the Palestinian Territories. Selma Hasan was amongst them. She had worked in Tunis as translator for Mahmoud Abbas, the chief Palestinian negotiator in Oslo. Naturally she was excited about visiting sites in Palestine. One winter morning Penny and I were planning to take a walk in the Dead Sea area and invited her to come along with us.

She had described the apartment block where she lived in some detail but we had a hard time finding it. During these two years since the signing of the Peace Accords with Israel, Ramallah, confined within the area allowed by the Israeli-approved town plans, had grown substantially. It was becoming more cluttered and shabby as new tower blocks built to house the newcomers were crammed within a small area of land. It did not help that the town was bathed in winter fog so thick I could hardly see my way.

When we finally arrived at Selma's place ten minutes late we found her waiting at the street corner outside, freezing. Between chattering teeth, she managed to say that she never knew Ramallah would be so cold.

'What did you expect?' I asked. 'It's higher than Jerusalem. The temperature is always at least one or two degrees lower.'

'But the fog, and the humidity. It's like living by the sea. Tunis was much warmer but this fog today reminded me of some of the winter days there.'

'We're open to the sea. There are no buffers. If you look on a clear day from the roof of your building you would be able to see all the way to Tel Aviv. It isn't really that far.'

'However much I read about this place and heard from people and looked at photographs I could never picture it.'

'Were you never here? Not even before 1967?'

'My family is from Safad and after 1948 we ended up in Beirut. I never visited the West Bank.'

She then added that in 1974 she joined Fatah, the main Palestinian resistance movement. She had lived a life so different from mine. Her husband, Isam, was a military commander with Fatah who now supported the peace between Israel and Palestine. He could not return to the West Bank without Israeli approval, which was taking a long time to be processed. I asked her whether there was any indication when he would be coming.

'He's still waiting for his Israeli permit in Amman. But you know how they are, they promise and then renege. I have been living on my nerves, preparing the apartment but not knowing whether we will ever live in it together. It's the worst state to be in.'

'Would you stay if he is not allowed to come?'

'I've been thinking a lot about this. Every morning I wake up missing him yet feeling so fortunate to be back in Palestine. The new re-created Palestine. I never thought I would live to see the day.'

I listened with annoyance at Selma's false idealism but kept my mouth shut. We had to stop at the first checkpoint on the road to Jerusalem.

For newcomers like Selma the natural history of this place begins in the present. She would not know, unless I pointed it out, that until a few years ago there was no barrier between Ramallah and East Jerusalem, which were then almost one city. So a reluctant pedagogue, I felt duty-bound to explain all this to Selma. At the same time I resented the fact that I had to be the guide and preferred to nurse my own thoughts and feelings as we travelled first to Jerusalem.

I never imagined the West Bank could be closed off from Israel. But how short memory is! I grew up when Jordan was in control. There was a strict border with Israel and I could never visit the 1948 areas of Palestine which had become Israel. But since the occupation of the West Bank in 1967 and the removal of the borders with Israel

I began to think of the country as one. Now new borders were being marked out unilaterally by Israel, ones that did not follow the historic green line between the West Bank and 1948 Israel.

As we descended towards East Jerusalem by the Sheikh Jarrah neighbourhood I realized that the beautiful Dome of the Rock, for many centuries the symbol of ancient Jerusalem, was no longer visible. It was concealed by new construction. This was by design. Not only had Israeli city planners obstructed the view of this familiar landmark – they had also constructed a wide highway along the western periphery of Arab East Jerusalem restricting its growth and separating it from the rest of the city. Highways are more effective geographic barriers than walls in keeping neighbourhoods apart. Walls can always be demolished. But once built, roads become a cruel reality that it is more difficult to change. No visitor would now sigh, let alone fall on his knees as many a conqueror and pilgrim in the past had done, upon beholding the Old City nestled between the hills. Now contorted, full of obstructions, walls and ugly blocks, it is a tortured city that has lost its soul.

We drove through a tunnel that burrows beneath Mount Scopus, shortening the distance between the settlement of Maaleh Adumim and West Jerusalem. Then just after we began our descent into the Ghor ('depth'), the Arabic name of the depression in which the Dead Sea lies, the settlement itself came into view. It was built over the site once occupied by the great Byzantine monastery of St Martyrius. The name of the settlement means the red ascent, after the colour of the rocks. It had started as a temporary labourers' camp for an industrial park being built there. Low retaining walls intended not to block the view encircled the heights. The instruction given by the

Israeli government to the town planner who designed the city was to build a town that was 'as big as possible'. This was scrupulously followed and the settlement that was created now has a larger municipal area than Tel Aviv. The architect's plan was to treat the hills over which the town was built as resembling the palm of a hand. He placed the town centre in the middle with the terraced houses serried on the 'fingers'. The valleys in between remained open. The general plan of the town was of a series of rings mounting each of the hills with those living inside never having to cross the internal roads. The slopes by the road were dug out to stagger them and prevent an avalanche of rock, soil and debris from the heavily worked heights. The building of this settlement was part of a plan, initiated by Golda Meir's government in the 1970s, to 'strengthen the capital'. Thirty years on Jerusalem has grown from a compact city of 37 square kilometres into a huge metropolis spread over 120 square kilometres. But the intention to increase the Jewish population in relation to the Palestinian did not work. Over the past two decades 300,000 Jews have left the city because of its poor planning, keeping the proportion of the Arab to the Jewish population steady.

A Scottish writer, William Dalrymple, gave an apt description of Maaleh Adumim as 'Milton Keynes transported into the landscape of a medieval Italian fresco'. The settlement had destroyed for ever that dramatic confrontation which had defined the physical and historic environment of the Holy City between the arid barren land and the fertile populated region. This was what gave Jerusalem its uniqueness as the last outpost of human civilization before the wilderness.

The old Jerusalem–Jericho road we used to take until

recently has a history dating back thousands of years. According to the Gospel, Jesus passed along it, stopping in present-day Azariah (Bethany) to raise Lazarus from the dead. A series of monasteries and churches mark Jesus' last journey to Jerusalem. Before the Israeli government built the wall that separates parts of the West Bank from Israel and annexes others, we travelled through East Jerusalem along the old city wall up to Ras El Amoud, where the view of the old city with the glittering golden Dome of the Rock mosque was spectacular. Then the descent to Jericho began along winding narrow roads. After Azariah and Abu Dis there was only a turbulent sea of yellow hills more like moon craters with a thin shaving of green growth during the late winter months if the rain happened to be plentiful. This central region of the West Bank is described as a plateau but is actually formed of horizontal layers that have been gently folded, a denuded ridge in which strata lean against each other, dipping in opposite directions. During the secondary era of geological time a period of folding occurred which resulted in the central hills of Palestine being lifted above the level of the sea. The folding was less severe in the south, where the ridges were simple though often of immense size. If one compares the topography to a groundswell produced by a storm at sea then the waves in the north were large, frequent and confused but in the south more gentle with a greater distance between them. That same subterranean phenomenon can be seen above ground. How like the sea these folds of hills we were passing were: waves with great troughs between them, until you approached the escarpment at the end of the Jerusalem wilderness that formed a great high wall bordering the Ghor.

The dual-carriage road to Jericho used to be winding and dangerous, as it should be, cutting through the wilderness connecting the ancient city of Jerusalem high up on the hills with the oasis of Jericho, the oldest town on earth and the lowest, lying 258 metres below sea level. Just after the ruins of the El Khan El Ahmar ('the Red Khan'), which is also referred to as the Inn of the Good Samaritan, I used to wait when I was a child for the cave by the side of the road. When he was not in a hurry, my father would stop the car and I would get out and quickly scramble up the small hill and look down. Except for the first few steps, which were lit by the light from outside, the rest was dark. As I concentrated on the cave the sound of traffic behind me would disappear in the background. It was said that this cave had stairs leading all the way to Jericho. But even in my imagination I did not dare go beyond the threshold and wander deep into this forbidding opening. I would remain standing precariously on the slippery slope, totally mesmerized, until my father's impatient calls broke through the silence and sent me hurrying back to the car to avoid upsetting him.

To make the road run straight and do away with its many curves, the new Israeli-built highway now cuts through the hills. I have no idea of the fate of the cave. It has probably been blocked by an Israeli bulldozer using mouthfuls of debris from one of the butchered hills. I also missed the coloured strata that flowed like veins through the rocks: brown, charcoal, purple, dark red and yellow. With the hills massacred you could no longer see the layers of rock. The colours seemed to have run, staining with swabs of pigment the exposed sides of the rocks through which the road ran.

'I never thought the Jewish settlements we heard so much about would be like this,' Selma announced from the backseat.

'How did you think they would be?' I asked.

'Temporary dwellings just to mark a presence, not like these stone houses with gardens and trees. They look so permanent and huge. What's the population of this one on the hill up there?'

'Maaleh Adumim must have something like 25,000 people by now.'

'This is almost as big as Ramallah.'

'The PLO waited too long. Negotiations should have started a long time ago. It only got more complicated with time.'

'As if the PLO didn't try. It was Israel that refused to negotiate with us,' Selma said, her voice betraying her annoyance with my self-righteousness.

My mind strayed again to the Master Plan, as it sadly is wont to do at moments when I'm enjoying the landscape. Israel had planned to settle 80,000 Israeli Jews in the central region of the West Bank by 1986. Despite huge economic incentives only 6,000 had been convinced to settle by the target date. But under the Oslo Agreements the PLO agreed to keep an area equal to about a third of the West Bank, referred to as Area C, outside the jurisdiction of the Palestinian Authority. It did so without questioning Israeli claims that most of this area was public land. Israel presented this to its public as tacit recognition by the PLO that the land, most of which Israel had already registered in the same Land Authority where Israeli state land is registered, would remain with Israel. This gave the settlement project a great boost. The average Israeli citizen came to believe that agreement had been reached with the PLO to designate Area C for Israeli settlements. They felt safe enough to invest in the settlements and move their families to them.

I told Selma what I thought of the Agreement.

'Don't be rash in your judgement,' she said. 'The Agreement might not be perfect but it gives us a footing on the land. Once the PLO is here everything will change. You just wait. These are new times.'

For the first time I felt like those Palestinians who stayed in Israel in 1948 must have felt when they argued with us after the 1967 war. They would tell us: 'You don't know a thing about Israel. We can tell you what is coming: land expropriations, biased zoning that will strangle your towns, and unfair taxation that will impoverish you.' And we would look with condescension at them and think they had lived for so long under Israel that they had become colonized, unable to think beyond their narrow claustrophobic reality. They probably think Israel is the whole world, we would comfort ourselves. Not only have their lands been colonized but their minds as well. Who wants to listen to the vanquished?

For twenty-five years I had studied the development of the Israeli sovereign legal language in the West Bank. I monitored how the Israeli state was being extended into the Occupied Territories through the acquisition of land and its registration in the Israel Land Authority. How large areas were being defined as Israeli Regional Councils and included within Israel. How the planning schemes were changed, how one area after another became to all intents and purposes annexed to Israel, and our towns and villages were left as islands within those Israeli extensions, fulfilling Ariel Sharon's promise made in the early eighties that Israel was going to leave 'an entirely different map of the country'. It was all done ostensibly through 'legal' manoeuvres, using the law in force in the West Bank because formally speaking the West Bank was not annexed to Israel. To understand and fight this was my war.

We passed an Israeli army jeep that had stopped a number of Palestinian cars. Soldiers were checking documents; one driver had been made to leave his car and stand by the side of the road. Selma was surprised: 'Aren't we in the Palestinian Territories? What right does the Israeli army have to stop Palestinian cars?'

I tried to explain that, under the agreements, Israel retained jurisdiction over the roads, then added: 'Do you know that the entire scheme for the new roads serving the settlements was being challenged and for many years the Israeli courts could not rule on the matter? After Oslo they closed the case with a short ruling to which no one paid any attention. So many new roads are now being built in our land for the benefit of settlers. There are no legal challenges even when we are prevented from using these roads. Do you happen to remember the memo I wrote the leadership about Road Scheme Number 50?

'Your memos were hard to translate,' Selma told me. She complained that my sentences were too long.

In his memoir, Mahmoud Abbas, the principal Palestinian negotiator at the Oslo talks, writes that he believed the delegation in Washington, which used English as the language of communication, was too concerned with words. To cut through all this crap, he went into secret negotiations in Oslo with the Israelis that ended with the signing of what came to be known as the Oslo Accords. The Palestinian negotiators at Oslo did not seek legal advice.

All the valuable experience and knowledge of Israeli legal manoeuvres gained from years of monitoring and challenging Israeli tactics were dismissed simply for reasons of style. The message was clear: the only struggle that was recognized was that carried out by the PLO outside the Occupied Territories. Like Selma the PLO negotiators did not have a real sense of what the settlements were about. And so the Accords the PLO signed saddled us with the Israeli legal and administrative arrangements that envisioned an unequal division of the land between Arab and Jew.

'Did you ever seriously believe your legal challenges could have forced Israel to stop its new road system let alone the settlements?' Selma asked me from the backseat, her voice patient but strained.

'Perhaps not but then Israel could not claim to be acting legally.'

'Big deal!'

Spurred on I said: 'And all these illegal military orders issued by Israel in the course of the occupation which the Agreement consolidates?'

'What military orders? The occupation is over. Can't you get it into your head that these are new times?'

As we drove further down to Jericho we passed the fledgling new settlement of Mitzpe Jericho. The language of conquest was writ large over the hills, over the wilderness, in every corner of the land. Everything signalled our defeat – from the earlier rows of settler apartment blocks piled over the dry pink hills forming the city of Maaleh Adumim to this latest settlement venture in the wilderness. When I travelled with our delegation through this area during the period of negotiations in Washington, DC, on our way to the Allenby Bridge across the River

Jordan, none of these settlements were here. They had doubled since the Oslo Accords were signed.

I couldn't help myself; I had to evoke the Master Plan. I said: 'Do you know that the Master Plan for this area calls for the extension of the Jewish settlements almost to Jericho? The wilderness from Jerusalem to Jericho would all be settled.'

'So? Have we not got jurisdiction? We can use it to annul them.'

'Then you haven't read the agreement and don't know Israel if you think it can be so easily tricked.'

'Why be so worried about the settlements?' Selma asked. 'We too will expand. Investments will pour in and we will create a new reality. You just wait.'

'How can we when Israel retains control over most of the land?'

'We'll work on what we have. Buy homes in the settlements and turn everything on its head. Remember these are new times.'

I was beginning to be annoyed by Selma's repetition of her 'new times' mantra. Her words kept echoing inside my head trapped by the clogging of my ears as we continued to descend to the lowest point on earth. New times indeed, I thought to myself looking out of the window at the sprawling new settlements invading the once bare hills.

I kept track of our descent by reading the blue tiles stuck into the rock marking the depth we had reached. The first read 200 metres above sea level. As I drove, my mind strayed, over the extent to which Selma was unaware of the destruction of the Palestinian legal case by the Oslo Agreements and what this meant for our future. The next strip of tiles read 'Sea Level'. I glimpsed it just as we reached the turning in the road before the hills parted to reveal the first view of the Dead Sea. For decades a Bedouin has stood at this point, with his camel colourfully saddled, waiting to give tourists rides over the once pristine wilderness, a fixed tableaux in a fast-changing universe. Selma excitedly pointed him out to us. There was pride in her voice, as though she had made a discovery. Perhaps she saw him as a symbol of Palestinian *sumoud* ('steadfastness'), proof that we were still masters over these lovely hills. How could anyone be so irresponsible as to express pride in a dreary time like this? Could she really be unaware that the Palestine she had returned to had not been liberated? How could she not see this?

We were 405 metres below sea level when we reached the Dead Sea, the lowest point on the earth's surface. We could not descend any further.

As a child I used to cast my eyes across the elusive divide between the West Bank and Israel. The town was here and over there were the hills with usurped Jaffa on the horizon. And nothing was in between. No roads, no development, no buildings. I never thought it possible to extend electricity lines and water pipes and establish human settlements in such faraway areas. Palestinians in the West Bank then did not have the technical or financial resources to undertake such projects. I had never seen it done; nor for that matter had I ever seen a bulldozer. After 1967 Palestinians needed a permit from the Israeli authorities to own one. When Israel began establishing settlements, opening roads through the hills, flattening hilltops and connecting far-flung places with water and electricity I was filled with awe. And fear.

The countryside I grew up in was being transformed

so rapidly I could hardly keep up. With large capital infusions from the US it was possible for the state of Israel to make the 'desert' bloom with concrete and neon lights. Vast areas of my beloved country were being fenced to become off limits to us. I felt the gravity of what was happening and I was willing to give everything for the struggle to stop it. My weapon was the law. All my time was taken up with it. Nothing was more important. I had no doubt that if we tried hard we would win and justice would prevail. For that glorious day of liberation there was no limit to what I was willing to sacrifice.

Now, after Oslo was signed and the struggle as I saw it was betrayed, I was back to real time. And with its re-entry into my life, my dead father's reproachful voice was also returning. He was still angry with me, disappointed at how my life had gone, asking unsettling questions: Why have you wasted your life? Why were you so distracted that you never raised a family? I knew the answer: when I was young I was too captured by the fear of the future to think of having children. I had no regrets. I was perfectly happy in my marriage. Yet I was in too weakened a state to stop him from ranting. He went on inside my head: What has your struggle achieved? Where did it get you? You never listened to me when I predicted the future.

We had reached the promontory just below the site of Khirbet Qumran overlooking a clear blue sea. This rift in the solid rock before which I now stood has not always existed. There was a time when this area was part of the 'supercontinent' of Africa, Florida, South America, Antarctica, Australia, India, Tibet, Arabia, Iran and southern Europe known as Gondwana. Geologists tell us that there was so much pushing up of the solid block of this land area that the strain crushed it, creating the rift valley that extends from north Syria down to East Africa, before which I stood.

The tourist authorities in Israel delineated with ropes and small placards the site where the Essenes had lived two centuries before Christ, pointing out how this renegade community survived, where its adherents met, ate and wrote, and how they collected and stored water and managed agriculture. They were the rebels of their day, the settlers who broke away from the ruling establishment and created their own settlement in the harsh conditions by the Dead Sea, where they managed to live by their own laws and practices. They wrote down their own interpretations of the Scriptures. Before the Romans destroyed their community in the first century AD they had managed to hide these texts in long jars in the deep caves, where they remained until a Palestinian shepherd looking for a missing goat entered one of the caves and discovered the clay jars with the scrolls still intact.

Today's Jewish settlers, not unlike the Essenes, appear to think of themselves as renegades breaking away from the ruling establishment and following their own beliefs and interpretations of the Scriptures. When you see them on street corners with their bushy beards, long hair topped by the knitted yarmulkes, fringes swaying beneath brown shirts and dusty sandals, you can get a sense of how anachronistic they are, like a people from another era. But unlike their predecessors these present-day rebels live on state subsidies. They are protected by the strongest army in the region and needn't work for a living. Instead they spend their time studying scripture in strategically positioned *yeshivot* (the plural of *yeshiva*, a Jewish religious school), which use the pretext of religious study to metamorphose into Jewish settlements that serve political objectives. Their heroism is attributed to their harassment of unarmed Palestinian civilians: women, men and children whom they attempt to drive away from the land they consider theirs. What will today's settlers leave for posterity but ugly structures which destroyed the land they claim to love and a legacy of hateful colonial practices condemned the world over that have contributed to delaying the onset of peaceful relations between the Palestinian and Israeli people?

I turned to look at the crystal-clear sea below the escarpment where I stood. I could not help recalling that it is one of those great marvels of the world which is in danger of disappearing. Over the years it has been shrinking at an alarming rate. Fifty thousand years ago its surface was at least 200 metres above the present level, which would mean that, standing on this promontory near the ruins of the Qumran settlement, the sea would be lapping at my feet instead of where it is now, almost a kilometre away. Even at the beginning of the twentieth century the sea was twelve metres higher than it is now. More recently the water has been declining by about a metre every year owing to Israel's diversion of the River Jordan and the tributaries which used to flow into it, and to the use of the seawater by factories in Israel and Jordan. Our precious land was slipping from under our feet as the Dead Sea was receding from its salty shores. The agreement that was branded as 'the peace of the braves', as Arafat was fond of repeating in his unique English, was nothing but a surrender document, a false promise for a better future.

I don't know why the memory came as I stood looking over the endangered sea. My father had told me many years ago that after he was forced out of Jaffa in 1948 he had continued to pay rent for his apartment there. Irrespective of the fact that he could not return to his home and had to scrimp for money in Ramallah, where he had no house of his own, the rent was due and had to be paid. This was the kind of man he was, conscientious and honest to the bone. I began to work out how old he was when the *Nakbeh* (the 'catastrophe', which is how Palestinians describe the loss of Palestine in 1948) struck and he lost everything he had worked for, his law office, his matrimonial home, and the lands he bought around Jaffa for investment. According to my calculations he was in his early forties, the same age as me now.

Within the short space of two decades my father had to deal with not one but two major catastrophes. After Jaffa he had re-established his home and office in Ramallah, which then came under Israeli occupation. For several years after 1967 he had little work. He was so distressed by the thought of losing everything once again that he considered ending his life. He put his shotgun to his temple and was about to pull the trigger.

At the last moment my mother stopped him and within a few days he was on his feet again. He switched from despondency to hyper-activism as he began to call for political realism, for the recognition of Israel and the establishment of a Palestinian state alongside it in all the Occupied Territories. He made his proposal before any Jewish settlements had been built in the West Bank and the Gaza Strip, before the rise and political empowerment of the religious right in Israel. How much suffering could have been spared had his call been heeded.

Nothing can be done to change the past but I knew I had to come to terms with the present. The truth was that we had been defeated. We had lost. For now the Israeli policies had succeeded. And I had wasted many years working on an area of law and human rights that came to nothing. Father lost his work twice. I lost mine only once. After years of hard work in the human rights field I was at the height of my career. Now the new political developments had made me redundant, unable to make any practical use of my legal knowledge and expertise to stop Israeli violations of the law.

I refocused on my surroundings. The western slopes of the Dead Sea are composed of beds of limestone with dark nodular pebbles that make the walk up to the Qumran Caves hazardous. I saw Penny and Selma charging ahead as I made my slow way up, alone. I continued to think of my father. He dedicated most of his life to the public good yet all his work came to nothing. He saw clearly what Israel was doing. He wrote and spoke about it, but the Palestinian leadership outside took no notice. They saw him as a political rival. Their primary concern was to keep all the cards in the hands of the external leadership. Political expediency blinded them to the war of annihilation Israel was waging against all Palestinians inside and outside the Occupied Territories. At the end of his life he was angry, frustrated and embittered. He used to tell me: someday you will know what I have come to know. I had done my best not to get infected by his lethal despondency. But with the onset of the Oslo period, when it became evident that it had indeed all turned out as he had foreseen, his admonishing voice returned with a vengeance.

Halfway up the hill I began to feel dizzy from the height and had to sit down. I could go no further. I seemed to be constantly slipping. I put both my hands on the ground and held firm for I felt I could easily tumble all the way down the deeply channelled side of this precipitous mountain into the abyss, with no way to stop my fall. With my hands anchoring me to the ground I turned my head and looked up at the unreachable caves. I could see their dark openings in the rocks. I wanted so much to stand at their mouths and look down into them as I used to do with my cave alongside the old road when I was young, travelling with my father to Jericho. But having sat down I could not make myself stand up again and continue the climb. I was petrified of slipping.

A black hawk was gliding low, not far from where I was sitting. He circled round and round. He seemed so dizzyingly close. Then a shadow began to slide across the mountain where I sat: a thick cloud had covered the sun. I felt the ground on which I anchored myself tilting.

Slowly and carefully, keeping close to the earth, I made my way down, almost crawling. Once at the bottom, I stood up and waited for Penny and Selma, who seemed to be taking their time. I didn't mind waiting. I relished the security of standing on level ground. The sea spread before me, so perfectly blue and sparkling. Usually seawater contains from 4 to 6 per cent of solids. The imprisoned waters of the Dead Sea hold more than 24 per cent. With the sun beating on me with such fierce heat I dreamed of plunging into water that looked as clear as day. But I knew better. This is not water for diving. It has a nauseating taste, feels oily and when it dries on the skin leaves a crust of salt over the body. If a drop of water touches the eyes they itch terribly, if it enters the lungs it can lead to death. Despite this, no other lake appears more blue and inviting. How could Mark Twain, when he visited this area in the nineteenth century, not have noticed its outstanding beauty?

Of all the lands there are for dismal scenery, I think
Palestine must be the prince. The hills are barren, they
are dull of color, they are unpicturesque in shape. The
valleys are unsightly deserts fringed with a feeble vegeta-
tion that has an expression about it of being sorrowful
and despondent. The Dead Sea and the Sea of Galilee
sleep in the midst of a vast stretch of hill and plain
wherein the eye rests upon no pleasant tint, no striking
object, no soft picture dreaming in a purple haze or
mottled with the shadows of the clouds. Every outline
is harsh, every feature is distinct, there is no perspective
– distance works no enchantment here. It is a hopeless,
dreary, heart-broken land.

(The Innocents Abroad)

The midday sun had turned the mountains to the
south into translucent sky-blue humps with their frizzled
edges silhouetted against the sky. Lit now from the back
by the afternoon sun the peaks closer to me overlaid the
ones further south with their edges marked by a dark
line. Both in colour and in texture what could be seen in
the distance was quite unlike the mountains when seen
close up, with their mud cliffs and stark scrub.

The tentative midday moon high up in the sky looked
as fleeting and flimsy as any slice of cloud. It reminded me
of those evenings we used to spend as a family on these
shores, before the Israeli occupation, with the music-
loving Georges, a Palestinian family originally from Haifa
who were forced to leave their home in Tiberius in 1948
and now lived in Ramallah. There was nothing like being
by the Dead Sea on the evening of a full moon. Usually
the George daughters played the accordion but it was
deemed too harsh an instrument for a romantic moonlit

evening so they brought their guitar and played more gentle music instead. I recalled one night when the moon was a particularly bright silver. The gently rippling sea managed to calm even as anxious a person as my father. We rented a boat and slid through the oily water in the dark, crossing the path lit by the moon.

Now the Lido Hotel next to which we spent that memorable evening was a long way away from the water, an abandoned miserable place. The sea has receded, leaving chunks of salt rock scattered along the coarse sand. Evaporation is incessant: every twenty-four hours as much as 25 millimetres of water evaporates from the surface of this small sea, leaving behind yet larger chunks of salt. But this was not what accounted for the high concentration of salt. Nor could it be explained solely by what the River Jordan brought down as it flowed into the lake. These salts were not the Jordan's own, but those of an earlier era reactivated by the washing action of the river.

On the Jordanian side of the Dead Sea, the banks rise steeply, forming a line of terraces that reach up as much as 3,000 feet above the shore, and composed of sandstone capped by limestone. They are deeply furrowed by the courses of the streams which descend from the high-level springs of the tableland and the fierce winter rains. With the sun shining on this wall of stone it turns into the most luminescent rose pink. As I looked across I remembered the walk Penny and I had taken during one of the breaks from the negotiations in Washington, DC, in the Nabatean city of Petra, on the southern edge of the sea. There are great walks to be had in that rose-pink ancient city. After an hour's walk through the barren deep ravine they call the Sik, bordered on both sides with rocks of different colours that change their hue depending on the angle the sun hits them we came to the imperious structure called the Treasury, made of decorated columns carved into the rocks. It was but a facade and yet it was so awe-inspiring that I felt like bowing before its towering beauty. After walking for weeks in the empty desert, the ancient traveller must have been overwhelmed when he came upon this delicate work of art. The whole of Petra is full of carvings on rocks that serve no apparent function except perhaps to impress and to awe. Not unlike the effect the Israeli settlements and their complicated network of roads, bridges and tunnels is intended to have on us Palestinians. Except that they are not just facades.

For many years I managed to hold on to the hope that the settlements would not be permanent. I had meticulously documented the illegal process by which they came to be established, every step of the way. I felt that as long as I understood, as long as the process by which all this had come about was not mysterious and the legal tricks used were exposed, I could not be confused and defeated and Israel could not get away with it. Knowledge is power. I had to keep up with the Israeli legal manoeuvres and expose them to the world. I had perceived my life as an ongoing narrative organically linked to the forward march of the Palestinian people towards liberation and freedom from the yoke of occupation. But now I knew this was nothing but a grand delusion. There was no connection outside my own mind between my knowledge and reality. It was only my way of feeling I was part of the rest of struggling society, a way of enduring hardships by claiming and holding on to the belief that there was a higher meaning to the suffering. That it wasn't in vain; it wasn't without purpose. As long as I was gaining a better understanding of the grand plan within which all this misery was taking place, my efforts had a point. I was not just a sufferer. I was an interpreter and challenger acting in solidarity with others.

But the Oslo Agreements buried my truth. The only resistance that was recognized was the PLO's armed struggle. The generally accepted claim was that it was the military struggle that was responsible for bringing us to this 'peace'. The legal battles waged for years against Israel were never recognized by the leadership, which, as I discovered, had the power to deny them at will. When the Oslo Peace Accords were signed I distinctly remember feeling the final rupture, the termination of what for years I had called my narrative. My bubble, my illusion, was burst.

And to make matters worse well-wishers from around the world were congratulating me that with the signing of the Oslo Accords and the famous handshake between Arafat and Rabin, shown countless times on CNN, 'good has finally won the day', a hope with which I had ended my first book in 1982 on life in the West Bank, *The Third Way*.

How baffled all this made me feel! How alone I found myself, standing on this promontory overlooking the Dead Sea contemplating the horrifying future and the end of a narrative of struggle I had thought I shared with others, which had given meaning to my life for so many years. As these thoughts passed through my mind I looked at the receding waters. An ecological disaster was looming here. The drop in the sea level, combined with the flow of fresh groundwater that dissolves the salt in the soil, was causing hundreds of sinkholes to appear along the shore. Some were as large as half a metre across and over 20 metres deep. It was no longer possible to walk here without fear of sinking into the salty sands. In the northern part of the sea, close to 200 sinkholes were appearing each year, making the entire area unsafe.

My silent musings were interrupted by Selma's mobile phone. It was a call from her husband telling her the good news that he had been issued a permit and would be crossing the bridge from Jordan tomorrow. She became so excited she started jumping up and down and ululating. Without a second thought, she decided to cut short her trip with us and return home in a taxi to finish her preparations for the house. Penny and I continued further south along the sea to the start of our main destination, the walk in Wadi El Daraj.

With Penny now driving I could look out of the window to my left at the perfectly still waters of the sea, transformed by the sun into a luminous platinum sheet, and to my right at the formidable wall of incandescent rock along which we were travelling, seemingly an impenetrable line of defence, a mighty gateway to another world.

Yet the variegated mudstone and marlstone surfaces were in fact friable. So vulnerable were they that it seemed possible they could collapse at any moment and disintegrate into the salt sea below. This side of the rift valley was streaked with coarse white strata of sandstone running through the silty mudstone. If you looked hard you could see all kinds of castellated shapes, pinnacles and turrets, colonnades and mounds of silt and shingle, carved by the salt-saturated wind blowing against them and smoothed by the water that cascaded from the tableland above.

We drove away from the main road by the Dead Sea,

up a narrow winding track, to get to the start of the walk marked on the Israeli guidebooks. We parked the car and began our hike on the black-marked trail. Even though we were quite high up and the trail was narrow, it was well marked and sensibly planned. I had no difficulty following it. As we walked on the sloping path the views of the valley were spectacular. It was a quarter of an hour before we got to the wide valley in the ravine. The sun was blazing down but it was pleasant with the high breeze. We lay down on the rocks for a brief rest. Before starting off again I wanted to see what was behind a narrow opening to the side of the valley and went to poke about in it. I saw a large crowd of youngsters, Israelis, who were sitting around on the rocks in a semi-circle listening to a lecture by their teacher about this gorge and its different features. They were doing their pre-military training, taking difficult walks and learning about the history, geology and military significance of different parts of the country. They were guarded by two armed soldiers, who stood at the front and rear of the group. The one near the opening eyed me with suspicion. When I left he followed me to make sure I was not up to trouble and was not going to harm the flock he was protecting.

I got back to Penny and we proceeded up the wadi. During flash floods its narrow mouth must have funnelled water with such force that anyone standing before it would be washed away and have no chance of surviving. We could see from the patina high up on the walls of the wadi the height the water had reached during the last flood.

We proceeded at a good pace and were eventually overtaken by the group of youngsters with the soldier guards I had seen earlier. We stepped aside and let them pass. They set about climbing up a rock that was so high they had to use a rope. When the last of the youngsters had ascended, one of the soldiers stepped back to let us pass. Penny went first. She was so nimble. She wrapped the rope around her feet and proceeded to propel herself up. When it was my turn I thought I too could do it. I clasped the rope with my feet and tried to imitate the action I saw Penny perform so easily, only to find myself unable to leave the ground. I tried other ways of doing the manoeuvre, to no avail. I began to regret not continuing with the Boy Scouts until I had mastered these skills. I would have remained stuck on the ground eying the rock with awe had it not been for the soldier, who proceeded to give me a push that almost sent me flying up that formidable rock. I couldn't but be grateful. Without him we would not have been able to proceed with our walk. In the course of this brief encounter the two of us did not exchange a single word. I wondered who he took me to be. Surely not a Palestinian.

We continued on our way. Now the valley was very deep but the path straddled the eastern side of the wadi and was not too difficult until we got to a point when we had to pass along a narrow passage that rounded a rock protruding from the cliff. It was not so narrow as to be absolutely impassable. Penny went first and was able to go around it without any trouble, but when I tried I found that I could not do it. There was no other way forward. Penny tried to explain how easy it was but she understood the irrationality of vertigo. She tried gentle cajoling to assure me that it was really not a difficult manoeuvre. She knew I needed time and left me to my own devices. I sat down and considered how I should best approach the task, knowing I could not go back. The walk was too long, we would be stuck in the valley in the dark and I would never be able to get down that high rock using the rope without help. I slowly approached the narrow turning and considered what would happen if I fell. I was sure I would not survive. What if my legs failed me? What if they refused to move? I would be stuck in the middle, holding on to the protruding rock for dear life. I yearned for a rope to wrap around my waist but we were not carrying such equipment. We thought of ourselves as walkers, not rock climbers. Perhaps this time we had chosen the wrong walk.

I stood above the cliff, looking down into the gorge, and began to fret again. I kept stretching my neck around the turn, and every time I saw that rock protruding I imagined that once I was in the middle it would somehow push me down. Or was it that I feared that I would jump? Did I trust myself not to throw myself down into that valley of death with its sharp rocks where I would have no chance of surviving?

I remained standing, forlornly examining this challenge and questioning my ability to meet it. Some thirty slow minutes must have passed with Penny standing on the other side waiting, patient and tolerant. Finally I forced myself to try. I clung to the rock, moving my feet ever so slowly, trying to keep my mind totally blank, feeling my heart pounding heavily in my chest. I do not know how I managed it but through repeating unthinkingly those mechanical motions that I had willed myself to perform, I found myself on the other side. Penny was on the verge of exasperation yet still managed to congratulate me for my bravery.

The rest of the walk was uphill but there were no other difficult parts. As we walked I had the chance to reflect on what had happened. I could now admit that objectively it was not a really difficult turn. It was true that the upper part of the rock was protruding over the path but the path itself was no less than half a metre wide. Nor did it project over a formidable drop. This part of the canyon wasn't as deep as it had seemed to me. Penny had passed it without difficulty, as must have all those Israeli young-sters doing their pre-military training. As I soon realized, what scared me most about this turning was something inside me.

The emotions were not too difficult to work out. The first was the old and persistent one of wanting a father, or an elder brother, to protect me. To catch me if I fell.

The second I interpreted as resulting from being at a point when my hold on life was being shaken. In the past I had lived with a strong sense of mission. What had framed my existence and given it a heightened sense of purpose was my resistance to the occupation, my work for justice. I felt called upon to save something, to speak out the truth, warn, resist and win. Now my struggle had been brought to an end. Consequently I lost the confi-dence that I wouldn't let myself fall to my death. The failures and disappointments I had been going through these past few years had loosened my grip on life and made me almost suicidal.

We had reached the end of the cliff walk and were walking on level ground to get to our parked car when we saw the Israeli bus that had come to pick up the young-sters. As they passed on their way to the bus I looked at their faces, flushed with confidence and joy. They spoke to each other in Russian. They must have been the sons and daughters of new immigrants brought to Israel to inhabit the settlements established on Palestinian soil.

They looked and acted as though the world belonged to them, for theirs was the new life of victory in war; ours the sour grapes of defeat. Amongst them I recognized the soldier who had given me that crucial push up the rock. He waited to see that all of his charges got on the bus and then firmly closed the door.

4

MONASTERIES IN THE DESERT

Wadi Qelt to Jericho

By the end of the nineties the future seemed to be only moving to bloodier times. This had been heralded by the increased rate of Israeli settlement and road building, the closing off of parts of the West Bank to Palestinians, settlers' attacks on Palestinian civilians and the brutal killings of civilians by Palestinian human bombers inside Israel. The brief respite that followed the first Intifada and the promise that prevailed during the first springs of the Oslo Accords, when each side watched the other with measured hope, soon passed and with it the freedom to roam freely the exquisite Wadi A'yn Faraa next to Wadi Qelt. It was essential not to hesitate but to venture out and take walks where it was still possible. And though most of upper Wadi Qelt, including the Faraa spring, was already closed to Palestinians, lower Wadi Qelt was still accessible.

The plan which Penny and I made with our friends Rema, Saba, another keen walker, his brother the doctor, and the brother's Russian wife, Maria, also a doctor, was to leave our cars in Ramallah, use public transport to Jericho and ask to be dropped halfway along the Jerusalem–Jericho road. From there we would walk down, passing by the old building which had once served as an inn for travellers on the ancient road between Jericho and Jerusalem. But the Israeli authorities were imposing another of those frequent sieges of Ramallah; the first obstacle was to be allowed out of Kalandia, the check-point separating Ramallah from Jerusalem.

There was a middle-aged soldier with a smiling face and round spectacles manning the post. He was too old to be a regular soldier and might have been a reservist, on duty in a dusty cubicle checking Palestinian identity cards. He first asked the doctor (who could enter because he had brought his medical identity card) to prove that the Russian woman next to him, who had forgotten to bring hers, was his wife. Then he decided that he couldn't let her pass.

'But why?' she objected. 'I'm a doctor and you're letting doctors through.'

'If I refuse to let you pass it would be a humanitarian problem. If I let you through I could be an accessory to murder,' the soldier proclaimed in his heavy accented English, looking pleased with himself, perhaps at being capable of such eloquence. Then he appeared to have another idea. He began to examine our friend's medical knowledge.

'Can you tell me where the sternum bone is?'

The Russian doctor looked askance at him. She seemed utterly baffled. Her light skin became pink, her long face seemed to grow longer and her eyes looked vacantly at her husband as she tried to understand this soldier's English.

'I can't understand,' she told her husband in Russian. She had very poor English.

The husband turned to the soldier and answered his question.

'I know you are a doctor. I want *her* to answer.'

Then he hurled another question at her: 'What disease is caused by the Epstein Barr virus?' he asked. Maria again looked confused while the husband tried to answer on behalf of his wife.

As this oral medical examination was taking place a whole line of people waited patiently, in silence. The rest of us also waited on the sidelines, too stunned, or perhaps fascinated, to intervene. The examination proceeded with Maria getting more embarrassed, on the verge of tears. She was desperately trying to decipher the questions of this middle-aged Israeli who spoke English in a strange accent. Meanwhile a Middle Eastern-looking soldier next to the round-faced one ordered all of us to go over to him. 'What's the problem?' he asked accusingly as if we were causing the delay. We told him that we were on our way to Jericho for a walk but his colleague had decided to conduct an examination of the medical knowledge of our friend the doctor. He turned and gave his colleague a patronizing look. He demanded we give him all the *hawieat* (identity cards). He put them together in one bundle, handed them back to us and let us pass, leaving the first soldier without the satisfaction of acting as a solo medical examination board.

After we passed the checkpoint I realized that I was seething with anger. Not at the soldier, but at myself. I, a lawyer, for many years a human rights activist, stood silently by and allowed this travesty to take place. More than any of the others who also stood by in silence I should have spoken up. What had happened to make me so passive that I made no attempt to stop the soldier from humiliating my friend? I was so grateful to the other soldier for saving us that I almost wanted to thank him. And what of the others? A motley crowd of Palestinians stood by as the soldier had fun at the expense of a respectable woman. Have we internalized defeat to this extent? Had this taken place before the Oslo Agreement I would have screamed at the soldier, demanded to see his superior, made it clear that he was exceeding his orders and made sure I put an end to my friend's ordeal. Instead we all stood by meekly, without so much as a whimper of protest and ended up feeling grateful just to have been allowed to pass. Perhaps it was time for me to leave.

My school friend Victor was amongst the first from my generation to decide that he would not be able to survive under the new regime. He had spent the best years of his life establishing a computer company under the most gruelling of circumstances, under the restrictions and obstructions of the Israeli occupation and the first Intifada. With the expectation of peace he had ambitious plans to expand his business regionally and had enough talented young people around him to manage this. One day he was called for a meeting along with other owners of computer companies to one of the Palestinian ministries that needed new software. They were asked to submit bids. He along with his staff worked day and night and produced the best offer. But they did not win the tender. A relative of the minister got it. This was a blow to Victor, who had pinned much of his hopes on this big job. This incident was followed by other depressing experiences of corruption and foul play. He sold programs to another ministry and did not get paid. He wondered how it was going to be possible to survive under the new regime.

One evening he came home from work and told his wife that the time had come for them to pack up and leave. They applied for emigration to Australia. They were both computer experts with money to invest. Their application was approved without difficulty. They had the brains, resources and skills. I visited them in their new country and found that they no longer bothered even to read the newspapers to learn what was happening here. They had made a complete break. And these were people who had been full of plans for developing the new Palestine. They had suffered the hardships of the first Intifada. They had ambitious schemes for outsourcing computer programs similar to those which helped Ireland and India revive their economies. All these plans had to be aborted because of short-sighted Palestinian officials drunk with power and determined to make quick gains. When I visited them in Australia, they seemed to have no regrets. Has my time to leave also arrived? Was the *sumoud* I had maintained for so long at an end?

We let the taxi drop us on the Jerusalem–Jericho road and scrambled down the mainly bare hills halfway between the two springs, Faraa and Qelt. We were going to start by walking upstream towards Faraa spring in upper Wadi Qelt, then wend our way back to the lower Wadi, visit St George's monastery, and continue to Jericho.

Wadi Qelt is a 25-kilometre-long wadi which has a greater abundance of water than most passable wadis in Palestine. The stream, which is strongest in winter, starts at A'yn Fawwar and empties into the River Jordan. When King Herod needed water for his winter palace in Jericho, he built the first aqueduct from A'yn Fawwar to

Wadi Qelt. During Jordanian rule a new aqueduct was built along the same route. Because of the availability of water, pilgrims and would-be conquerors have used the valley as a route to Jerusalem, Damascus and even faraway Baghdad.

The better start for the Wadi Qelt walk, the spectacular ravine that cuts down to Jericho from the eastern Jerusalem hills, is at A'yn Faraa, one of the main springs that feeds into the wadi. But the last time I was able to begin the walk from there was in 1993. It was still possible then for Penny and me to drive through the hills around Jerusalem until we reached the Jewish settlement of Almon, which had been established at the foot of the spring, not far from the Palestinian village of Hizma on the Ramallah–Jericho road, eight kilometres north-east of Jerusalem. We would park the car at the settlement, lock it and without fear of being shot at begin the walk in upper Wadi Qelt. Indeed, a nature sign still points the way to the settlement's car park – but no Palestinian would now be allowed to approach its barricaded entrance. The route along this path through the wadi descends from 640 metres to about 100 metres below sea level at St George's monastery and ultimately to minus 258 at Jericho. It crosses three ecosystems. Because of the constant flow of water from the three springs, Faraa, Fawwar and Qelt, the valley is home to a great variety of wildlife including foxes, rock hyrax, lizards, porcupines and a great variety of birds: herons, falcons, kingfishers, eagles and ravens. The water in the wadi stream has frogs, crabs and fish.

We had no trouble finding the path. Once in the canyon we visited the remains of what is claimed to be the first monastery in the Jerusalem wilderness, founded by the third-century hermit St Chariton. In 275 Chariton was on a pilgrimage from Jerusalem when he was abducted by bandits and brought to a cave in the Farra Valley. According to tradition the bandits were killed by drinking wine poisoned by a snake. After the miraculous death of his abductors, Chariton decided to stay in the cave as a hermit and was later buried nearby. Following a brief visit to the ruins we followed an old road to the British Mandate pumping station, surrounded by eucalyptus trees. Here was the beginning of the first-century BC aqueduct built by Herod which took water to the next spring, A'yn Fawwar, and from there to A'yn Qelt and on to the outskirts of Jericho.

The short walk down that meandering road brought us to the powerful A'yn Faraa spring. In the desert the contrast between the aridity of the surrounding area and the greenery in the Faraa Valley was striking, a reminder of the transformative power of water. It is at its most lush in late winter and early spring. By the middle of spring the wild flowers begin to dry up, much earlier than in the Ramallah hills, which are significantly higher.

Walking in this canyon we had the feeling of being in a large, deep basin with high rocks on both sides. That winter in 1993 the water had filled a section of the valley deep enough for a swim. It was a hot day but we decided against plunging in. Though we did not mention it we were both thinking of the murder of a Jewish settler in that same area by Bedouin boys a few months earlier. With her light-coloured hair and fair complexion Penny would be indistinguishable from a settler.

When we first arrived at the deep section of the wadi after following the curve of the rocks, we saw a large heron fishing. When he heard us he slowly flapped his wide, unwieldy wings and reluctantly flew up. He

perched on a high rock and waited for us to leave so that
he could finish his meal. I was sorry that he felt the need
to fly away on account of us. With the only sea close by
being the Dead Sea, it was rare to see a bird fishing in our
dry hills. I looked up at him and saw that on the rocks
just above where he landed were Bedouin shepherd boys
tending their flock of sheep. They too were watching us.
I gave them a friendly wave. I didn't see them wave back.
It was a tense walk during anxious times.

As soon as we left the taxi that brought us down close
to Wadi Qelt we found ourselves almost running over the
hills, which were like a brown tapestry. We felt euphoric.
Being stuck in Ramallah, surrounded as it was with
checkpoints at every exit, the experience of open space,
with no walls, no barriers and a wide open sky, made
us giddy with joy. We continued up the hillock until we
came to a promontory where we could see the canyon
stretched below and began our descent.

Our leader on this walk was Saba, hulking and
dishevelled, shirt-tails out and trouser legs sweeping the
ground. Early in the occupation, when he was still in his
mid-teens, the Israeli authorities expelled his father to
Jordan. He left behind his wife and two young sons. With
the father gone Saba was forced to assume responsibility
for the family. He resented the burden of having to act as
a parent to his younger brothers. Though many years had
passed he continued to feel bereavement over his stolen
youth. To his friends he is one of the most faithful people
I know. When he graduated from high school he left
Ramallah and joined the Palestinian armed resistance in
South Lebanon. He later spent time in Israeli prisons. But
he still managed to pursue higher studies in history in
Cairo and Paris. In his academic writings he showed the

same boldness that he exhibited in life by writing about topics that others shied away from, like the issues of collaboration and Israeli massacres that remain undocumented. His views on the principal PLO faction, Fatah, and its leader, Yasser Arafat, were revisionist. Though he made great strides in his academic career, that crucial absence of fatherly love and protection when he most needed them left him wounded, suffering a sense of inadequacy and a feeling of being underrated.

As we walked I observed how Saba approached the hills. I knew how much he loved walking in them and how he found himself in nature. But unlike me he never kept to the trail when one could be found. He clomped down over the terraces, causing stones to tumble and creating his own new paths. And when danger lurked it never deterred him. When we saw a pack of stray dogs ahead we were inclined to change direction. But not Saba. He marched right up to them and sent them packing.

But perhaps the biggest difference between the two of us was best exemplified by our respective responses to the second Intifada. For several months after it began I refused to recognize what was taking place. I continued to wish it away. Whereas he immediately thought it was bound to lead to our mass expulsion by Israel. For months and years he lived in fear of a second *Nakbeh*. Clearly his historical readings and personal experiences had worn him down.

The descent to the valley was quite steep. It was just the kind of walk Saba should lead for now there were no recognizable tracks that we could follow. We just scrambled down. In the water-filled canyon masses of the fragmite reeds were growing. We had been warned

143

of water snakes, so we avoided walking in the water. Eventually we found the track by the southern side of the canyon and followed it towards A'yn Faraa. We were determined to go as far as we could and only turn back when it became absolutely necessary to avoid confronting the armed guards from the settlement of Almon.

In this section, the canyon was deep and narrow. The large boulder walls twisted and curved, forming small basins. We walked along the narrow path, negotiating our way around rocks, some of which were as precipitous and unfriendly as in Wadi El Daraj, until we reached a wider part of the valley which was sheltered on both sides by very high cliffs. Below, the water was thick with reeds and spearmint. Further upstream the canyon bent sharply. The part of the valley behind this blind corner was totally concealed. I thought it might have been the point at which Penny and I had stopped when we were approaching the valley from the direction of Wadi Faraa. We found a spot by a large carob tree and had our picnic. The water streamed below where we sat.

Then we heard noises. We looked up and, below the escarpment at the opposite side of the stream, saw a number of settlers approaching. We assumed they were from Almon coming down to visit *their* spring next to where they lived. They must have seen us as trespassers, potentially dangerous but perhaps, by the way we looked sitting there drinking coffee and eating our salads, not quite people on a military mission. One of the girls from the group approached Rema and asked her: 'Where are you from?' Rema's answer was both straightforward and correct. She simply said: 'From here.'

The settler women wore long skirts and covered their hair. They continued walking on the narrow paths along the steep rock opposite us while we held our ground by the carob tree and tried to avoid looking at them. An uneasy sharing of the picnic ground proceeded with each side excelling in keeping watch without seeming to do so. When we finished our picnic we decided not to venture behind the blind corner. Times were such that it was better not to test our luck. We packed our provisions and proceeded eastward towards St George's monastery and Jericho.

Just as we were leaving I looked up the rock wall below which we had been sitting and saw a young woman with the long orthodox dress and headscarf standing reverently. Her face was turned westward; she had a calm pious expression. She was praying. I could not tell if she was an Israeli Jew or a newly arrived immigrant. In my many expeditions in different parts of the country I had never seen anyone praying, though I often thought of my walks in nature as a form of meditation. Oddly it was a flattering sight: here was someone who appreciated my land so much that she was inspired to give thanks to her God in prayer. And yet I could not help being suspicious of her motives. What was the nature of her supplication? Was she giving thanks to the Almighty for the glory of His creation or for His support of the Israeli army in their conquest and occupation of my land, making it possible for her to settle in Almon by the side of this spectacular spring? Religious practice in the Land of the Bible tends to encourage exclusivity and discrimination rather than love and magnanimity. There is no place like the Holy Land to make one cynical about religion.

After leaving the settlers we proceeded along a path that followed the contours of the rocks until we reached Fawwar spring. In Arabic the name means 'bubbling', from the fact that this spring gushes and stops at regular intervals like a fountain.

As we walked away from the sound of the water and came to a quieter section I noticed that Rema, who is an anthropologist, was scanning the horizon. When I asked her if she was looking out for settlers she said she wasn't. She was missing the Bedouins whom she used to meet and chat with on walks in this area. She knew a lot about the kind of life they led in this canyon, where they had grazed their sheep for years. Now they had been chased away by the Israeli authorities. 'It is as though the life had been sapped out of these hills,' she said. Most accounts by travellers who have walked in this area describe how they were struck by the bareness of the hills surrounding the lush valley and the preponderance of the Bedouin shepherds roaming them. Now only the bareness remained.

I thought of the absent Bedouins as I walked. Theirs was a different vision of the land. They saw it as an integral whole. In the summer they pitched their tents over high ground where it was cool, and in winter they descended to the Ghor to reduce the likelihood of their newborn goats and sheep dying from the cold. In a country where there has been such a scramble over land they hardly ever bothered to register any in their name. How could they when they didn't conceive of it as divisible plots?

The rocks where we walked were indeed strikingly bare, the water down below, which at first gushed over the boulders in the valley, progressively dried up until we reached the next spring, A'yn Qelt when the flow strengthened again. We could now see that the irrigation canal on the opposite side of the canyon through which we were walking was fed by the water of the spring. The valley here was wider. A short distance later we came upon a dirt road that branched off from the main Jericho–Jerusalem road, which in earlier, more stable times we used to drive down before parking our cars and walking to St George's monastery and back. There were a flour mill and a number of abandoned houses which belonged to the Husseini family. A dedication written in Arabic commemorated the restoration of the old aqueduct that took the water to the outskirts of Jericho as well as the building of a dam and the flour mill by one of the family.

Not far from this area was the attractive Nabi Mousa *khan* (inn for pilgrims), where according to Muslim tradition the Prophet Moses was buried. The *khan* had recently been renovated by the Muslim Trust, the Awkaf. Prior to 1948, every year around Easter, large numbers of people travelled from different parts of Palestine to this spot, where for three days and nights they took part in one of the most colourful festivals of the Palestinian calendar. Those attending the celebrations slept over at the *khan* or in tents pitched on the surrounding hills. In order to feed the crowds, the mill provided flour for making bread. It must also have serviced the monastery and the Bedouin tribes living nearby. Now this seasonal public event had come to an end and the Israeli Parks Authority controls a region subdued and sapped of its former vibrancy.

We crossed the stream and walked along the canal which followed the northern side of the valley until we reached the only inhabited part of this wadi. A few families were living in brick houses right by the canal, the last remaining Bedouins in the area. It was clear that they were not sure whether we were Israeli or Palestinian. With our jeans and T-shirts we looked foreign enough. We greeted them in Arabic and they invited us for tea. We sat on their porch next to the canal, overlooking the valley below. The smell of their *taboon*, where they baked bread, was enticing. Fatmeh, one of the two wives of the man of the family, provided the tea. Her married daughter, who sat with us, was holding on to her baby, refusing to let her go. Eventually two teenaged boys emerged but they spoke very little and spent their time casting curious looks at our group of mixed men and women. I noted that in response to a question about the number of children Fatmeh had, she mentioned that the family included two donkeys, which made us laugh. I was hoping to hear that the children were able to ride these beasts to their school in Jericho, at least a three-hour walk away. But they said they didn't. No such luxury for the kids. They had to make a daily trek to Jericho and back.

The two women soon disappeared into their kitchen and we realized they were bringing us food along with the tea. We tried to dissuade them from going to the trouble but they would not hear of it. We were their guests and guests must be treated generously.

We Arabs have traditionally glorified generosity. It is regarded as one of the traits of God and indeed in the Holy Qur'an it is one of His many names. It is also defined as the opposite of meanness. Like love, generosity in the Arabic sense is not calculating. It is giving without any expectation of reward. It is not doing what is expected. It is neither the opposite of penury nor could it be characterized as being a spendthrift. The famous case, which we all learned about in school, was that of Hatem, whose name has become synonymous with generosity, so that one says so and so has Hatem's generosity. He lived in a remote area and was once visited by travellers. He had no meat to offer them so he looked around and saw his camel, his only means of transport. He slaughtered it, offering its meat to his guests rather than send them off without a proper meal.

This glorification of generosity and trust in Arab tradition has sometimes been detrimental to ourselves. At crucial moments in our history, Arab leaders failed to look beyond the individual they were showering with kindness to the policy which he was serving. Thus many fell to the charm of those who came to colonize our land, whether they were British or Zionist Jews. More recently it was the Norwegians, newcomers on the international scene, who exploited this weakness by inviting the Palestinian negotiators to live with their Israeli partners in a residence situated in Norway's woods, where the children of the Norwegian officials were brought in to lighten the atmosphere. All this with the intention of making them gain each other's trust, as though the essence of the problem between us was one of lack of trust, not the colonization of Palestine! The Norwegians succeeded. The Oslo Agreement was signed, the settlements were not removed and the much-anticipated peace was not accomplished.

We sat on the Bedouin family's porch by the cement-lined canal with its fast-rushing water, sipping tea and enjoying their freshly baked bread and the quickly prepared meal they offered. Despite our sincere entreaties our hosts would not join us. It is improper, according to tradition, for the hosts to eat with their guests. The hosts' role is to watch over their guests as they eat and be attentive to their every need. After we had finished, and when Fatmeh learned that I was a practising lawyer, she brought a paper to show me. It was notice from the Israeli

Parks Authority that they had only one year left in this place, after which they must leave their home because the land had been expropriated and was being turned into a nature reserve.

There was a time, in the early years of the occupation, when I commended the military authorities for their contribution to the preservation of our countryside through such declarations. Then it became evident that they were doing great damage to the land and its flora and fauna through their extensive building of settlements. They were acting like a sovereign, re-shaping the countryside, exploiting empty land for the benefit of their own people and designating other areas as reserves for their future benefit. After 1967, when Israel occupied and then annexed East Jerusalem, my father lost many valuable plots of land when the Israeli municipality designated them green areas. I began to think Israel was going to turn East Jerusalem into a paradise of green parks, only to realize that a few years after the land had been acquired from its Arab ownership through expropriation, its designation was changed. The noble aim of keeping East Jerusalem green was dropped in favour of using the land to construct neighbourhoods for the exclusive benefit of Jewish residents, making the city more cluttered and depressing, and my father more despondent, than ever.

Fatmeh wondered whether there was anything they could do to hold on to their home. Her husband had been working for the Israeli Society for the Protection of Nature and his employment was also going to end. She pointed to the land just across from the valley and told us that the settlement of Mitzpe Jericho (in Hebrew, 'lookout over Jericho') was being expanded over the hill just above the ravine. Once this happened they would fence off the area and the entrance to the wadi would be controlled by the settlement. Only Israeli Jews and tourists would be allowed into the valley, there would be no need for the Bedouin employee to ward off incursions by Arab shepherds or walkers. This left me wondering from whom the Israeli Society was trying to protect nature.

Saba turned to me and said: 'I have always known it. The Israeli plan is to confine all of us in reservations in preparation for our eventual expulsion. Just as they did in 1948.'

I looked at his pinched face and realized that, more than any of us, he lived with the constant phobia of a repeat of the 1948 *Nakbeh*. History might not have been the best subject to specialize in for someone of Saba's melancholic temperament.

Throughout our stay the younger woman with the child had remained silent, holding her daughter close to her bosom. We asked how many children she had and noticed that she became tearful. She then told us about her young son, a baby just learning to crawl. She had left him on the porch to run inside for a few minutes to fetch some food, when he crawled into the canal and was carried away by the fast-flowing water. She ran after him but could not save him. She found him amongst the reeds and debris that had been trapped by a grating a short distance from her home, drowned.

We spent what we deemed was an appropriate period of time with them, so as not to offend this family who had treated us with such generosity, and then we were on our way.

After 1948 and the Arab exodus from Haifa, parts of the Carmel forest were designated as nature reserves. It was deemed that the greatest enemy of these forests was the goats owned by Arab farmers who had managed to stay in the country. Legislation was enacted, and firmly enforced, to restrict the grazing of goats in these protected areas. It cannot be denied that goats are not discriminating in what they eat. They have the annoying habit of climbing up tree trunks to munch on the green foliage, especially of young saplings, often leaving the grass below untouched. Over the years they have caused undeniable damage to the natural flora of Palestine. But any attempt to interfere with nature is not without its risks. In the Carmel forest the goats used to feed on the parasitic plant *hamoul* (Field Dodder), which is hard to control and nearly impossible to eradicate. Its thread-like, yellow stems wind themselves around the trunks of pine trees. With the banning of the goats from the forest the Dodder spread uncontrollably, so that when wild fires began, they spread more easily over a larger area. And just as the goats ate many of our beautiful wild flowers they also fertilized the land, invigorating the soil and ensuring that growth would be stronger in future years. They took but they also gave.

The Bedouin to whom Fatmeh and her family belonged, most of whom were conspicuous by their absence, were from the Jahalin tribe. They originally made their home in the Negev, where they lived their nomadic life in tents, raising their goats and occasionally occupying themelves with seasonal agriculture. In 1950 the Israeli army pushed them out and they re-established themselves at the edge of the wilderness, just by Jerusalem, on land that belonged to the Arab village of Abu Dees. They continued living there in their tents, moving eastward in winter to a warmer region, where they stayed until early spring, leaving only after their goats had given birth and the young had grown big enough to move on. But when in 1976 a handful of Israeli families founded the new settlement of Maaleh Adumim, the Jahalin had to be evicted again. They put up a protracted struggle to hold on to the land where they had been living for over two decades. The case went to the Israeli High Court, which, as usual, after taking its time, produced a long, carefully drafted, impressive decision that favoured the state. The policy of surrounding East Jerusalem with Israeli settlements was not subject to review for the sake of a Bedouin tribe. The state was kind enough, after keen media attention, to offer the deposed Bedouins an area near the municipal rubbish dump, from which, years later, they would once again be moved. Some noble objectives have to be realized whatever the human or environmental cost.

As we descended along the canal to Jericho, the valley became wider and more lush. We came upon fields of poppies which were taller and more plentiful than any that grew in the Ramallah wadis. Our path passed across aqueducts that stretched between the two sides of the canyon and which, because of my vertigo, I had great difficulty crossing. I would rather have walked down in the wadi but this would have taken much longer. My fear of heights must have become stronger as I had grown older. Certainly I did not remember having to put up such a struggle during earlier walks in the same area.

But I kept my fear to myself and tried not to let the others suspect what I was going through. If I succumbed I would have to give up the walk and miss the splendour of what was yet to come.

I saw Penny looking at my tomato-red, perspiring face with concern. She knew what I was feeling. I tried my best not to look down at the depths on either side of me.

I was filled with dread but kept telling myself I had to conquer my fear, that I must go on. I turned my head up to the blue sky. It always helps to concentrate on the good things, not to indulge oneself in despair or despondency. I thought of the cool air inside the attractive monastery that awaited us on the other side.

Slowly, by sheer strength of will and all the time putting on a brave face, I overcame my fear and made it across. I was wet with sweat and my heart was pounding. But I had done it. As we approached St George's Monastery the landscape became more dramatic, with higher, more raggedy cliffs. The canal straddled the rock walls quite high up the cliff. From my vantage point I could see a cross fixed to the ground at the highest point on the opposite cliff from where we walked, presumably to be visible to travellers on the Jerusalem–Jericho road and assert the holiness of this cursed land. The mystery and attraction of these areas lay in their remoteness and inaccessibility. During earlier walks all that I could see was the empty wilderness. Now the area looked like a construction site as the new roads to the settlements of Maaleh Mikhmas, Kfar Adumim, Mishor Adumim and Mitzpe Jericho were dug in the hills and land was levelled in preparation for building yet more houses there. Once these settlements are complete a wedge will divide the West Bank into a northern and a southern enclave and put an end to the dream of a Palestinian state.

The light was spectacularly clear against the rocks all around us. We walked without talking along the side of the canal in single file, keeping our thoughts to ourselves. There were no more sharp drops, so I could relax. Saba was leading, the Russian doctor was in front of me. She had been silent for most of the walk, reflecting, I presumed, on that distressing episode in the morning. We walked slowly for we were all tired.

In the silence and rhythm of my footsteps, I began to reflect on the course of my life over recent years. As long as I was engaged in the struggle I believed that international law, rationality and decency would ultimately prevail. The Jewish prophet Isaiah, who famously cried in vain in the wilderness, was supposed to have stopped here in this wadi on his way to Egypt. I too have been crying out in a wilderness, to a world that did not hear. Along with other committed Palestinians from the Occupied Territories I addressed the Israeli side and warned that the future would be bleak for all of us if these settlements were not stopped. I also went on speaking tours in the US, alone and with others, Palestinians and Israelis alike, to caution against a disastrous policy that supported and funded the settlement project. Isaiah so despaired that he begged for an end to his life without hope. I hoped I would never know such despair.

As we rounded a bend in the cliff we were no longer directly exposed to the sun. A quieting, relieving coolness came upon us as we walked in the shade. I remembered reading that it was this narrow and deep ravine that inspired the life-affirming words of Psalm 23: 'Even though I walk through the valley of the shadow of death, I fear no evil.'

As we approached the Monastery of St George of Koziba we noticed that the ground had been cleared of stones. The garden had a variety of trees: palm, olive, citrus, oleander and cypress. East of the wadi was a copse of pine and on a lower terrace a gorgeous palm spread its fronds in every direction. The trunks of two of the olive trees opposite the monastery had braided trunks, as though the roots had grown the wrong way, wrapping them-selves around the trunk rather than descending into the ground. The unusual trunk echoed the southern cliffs, which were castellated with round knobby columns of similar shape.

It has always struck me how gardens seem to have a life of their own. I could not see anyone working, not at this hot hour of the day. There is something irresistibly attractive about cultivating a garden in the depths of the wilderness.

The monastery hangs on a precipice in the north side of the wadi in the manner of other monasteries at the edge of the desert, such as Mar Saba near Bethlehem and Kruntal in Jericho. On either side along the rock wall were numerous caves, some with walls closing their openings, others with ladders which the hermits who had lived in them had once climbed. A small oratory built by five hermits in AD 420–30 was transformed into the Monastery of St George of Koziba by John of Thebes about 480. It was virtually abandoned after the destruc-tion visited on it by the Persians in 614 but was restored by Manuel I Comnenus in 1179. The monks who have lived here over the centuries have succeeded in secluding themselves from the successive waves of conquerors, some more brutal than others. They endured the heat of summer, the inevitable scarcity of provisions during years of conquest and famine, and the fear of attack from marauding armies and bandits. They managed their monastic life and kept their garden going.

After walking beneath the tall cypresses, oleander bushes and citrus orchards growing on both sides of the flowing stream, I was looking forward to going into the monastery, which consisted of a series of cells and a hall supported on vaults. I remembered how dark, quiet and cool was the interior of the church and how awesome were its famous icons. I crossed the bridge over the deep wadi and climbed the long wide stairs with high banisters until I got to the gate. I went up a narrow staircase with wrought-iron railings to a brown metal door that was closed. Most times I have been on this walk the monastery has been closed. Would it also be out of reach this time? I knocked once lightly with the circular metal door knocker. But no one came to the door. I waited then knocked again, harder this time. An old monk, in a brown habit and with a withered face, looked down from the balcony to see who was causing such pandemonium, disturbing the peace of this quiet place.

'Who is this? What do you want?'

I said I wanted to visit the church. He scrutinized my face then, to my relief, opened the door.

'But just for a short while,' he said.

I entered a small porch with stairs to the extreme right going up into what looked like private living quarters and another further along going down to a sort of crypt below the ground. The monk led me to the church. I entered the darkened chapel with icons all around and a faint smell of incense. It had an unusual design for a church with a peculiar orientation that followed the direction of the rock escarpment it abutted. The east window, beside the apse was at an angle of 90 degrees. Inside this darkened, twelfth-century chapel, I felt myself entombed by the rock firmly, securely dug in. There was a faded fresco on the wall and mosaic floors that were only half preserved. I walked through a corridor covered with frescoes representing the Last Judgement to a chamber cut out of the rock where a vault containing ancient bones was located.

This was the oldest part of the building. I looked at the icons; some were new but some very old. Two that were by the door attracted my attention. One had a holy cow with angel wings. I had never seen a cow memorialized in church in this way. Another was of a deer with a cross between its antlers and a monk looking on in awe. Perhaps a miracle had occurred in this wilderness when it still had deer.

When I left I was struck by the roughness of the exterior compared with the highly decorative inside of the church. There was a solidity and inviolability to this monastery built into rock. Had the monk refused to open the metal door there would have been no way for me to enter. To seek isolation, even in the wilderness, requires good planning and design.

In this land of turbulence and wars there have always been oases of tranquillity and peace where monks have been able to hide themselves away, never bothering with the worldly events taking place outside their door. This perhaps was the only saving grace of religion in the Holy Land. It occurred to me that I too should draw inspiration from this long tradition, and search for a tranquil place where I could take refuge and sit out the bad times, nursing my despair about Israel's unbridled power, until it is healed.

I cannot continue in this state of anger, otherwise it will consume all my energy and I shall waste my life in grumbling and regret. A time comes when one has to accept reality, difficult as that might be, and find ways to live through it without losing one's self-esteem and principles. Was this not what these hermits and monks had been doing over the centuries, keeping their distance from the world, holding on to what was theirs as they waited for the tide to turn, while around them all they held sacred was violated? The time had come for me to dedicate myself to a different project, one I could make work, which no one could take from me. Writing would help sustain me in this next period. But it was only honest and daring writing that would be able to penetrate the depths that enveloped and paralysed me now.

The wilderness behind Jerusalem is now mainly settled and the monks live in an area that has been declared a nature reserve. The changing times offer them yet another challenge among the many tribulations they have had to overcome during their long residence in this lonely valley. This time the transformation is permanent. Whatever the resolution of this intractable political conflict, this area will never return to being the wilderness it once was. Isaiah would not want his life back. As to the resilient monks, I have no doubt that they will survive as they have in the past.

We rested at the monastery garden, ate a few oranges, drank water and continued our walk to Jericho, the oldest continually inhabited city in the world. In the past it had survived on agriculture and the services it rendered to visitors from the hills who came to enjoy its mild weather and good restaurants. Now with the checkpoints blocking all entrances to the city, desperate unemployed young men living inside have found work helping to build the nearby settlements and working as day labourers in the Israelis' industrial zones. Not only was Israel re-zoning our land, it was determining our society's economic and social life.

At the end of the walk, as we were taking a shared taxi back to Ramallah, I looked out at the blazing mist over the western hills of Jerusalem high above the Ghor and thought to myself: What are you complaining about? Materially I had lost nothing. I still had my law office and my home. I had a happy marriage. I knew I would be able to find ways of dealing with the trauma of defeat. Somehow despite the problems and fears I would continue to walk and to write. At my age my father had successfully survived two catastrophic defeats. I was more fortunate. So far, I have had to deal with only one.

5

AND HOW DID YOU GET OVER IT?

Janiya, Ras Karkar and Deir Ammar

I had studied the Oslo Agreement well enough to realize it would lead to chaos. So I tried to take measures against what I was sure would be coming. I built my house within the borders of Ramallah, where I considered it would be safe from Israeli expropriation, and proceeded to cultivate my garden and write a book of memoirs, *Strangers in the House,* that I had long thought about. I was digging my heels in, taking refuge in a stone house and waiting for the tide to change, an honourable tradition in the Holy Land, where over the centuries so many missions, monks, and pockets of religious and ethnic groups founded monasteries, schools, or institutions, and confined themselves within their walls, or stood on pillars as they waited out the bad times. In the one *dunum* of Ramallah land on which Penny and I had built our house, we had an open courtyard in the centre where we also reserved for ourselves a piece of sky. Finding such refuge during bleak times was maybe the only way to preserve one's integrity and way of life. It was no surprise, perhaps a premonition, that when I was a child *The Spanish Gardener*, a story about a boy whose father wanted him to grow up protected within the confines of a beautiful walled garden and never to be exposed to the ills of the world, was my favourite tale.

Mustafa Barghouti and I had been friends for many years despite our being fundamentally different. He was a doctor and a politician. I, a lawyer and author. We were fond of taking walks in the hills and talking about current events and sharing our political analysis of how things were going. We had started our professional lives at almost the same time, in 1978. He founded the Medical Relief Organization and I the human rights organization Al Haq. For many years we were neighbours and had many opportunities for long talks, as we walked in the hills behind where we lived. We would discuss the role of civil society in resisting the occupation and the establishment of non-governmental organizations such as the ones we had started in the late seventies. Both were pioneering organizations that had played significant roles in their respective fields and had promoted alternative forms of civil struggle against the occupation, especially during the first Intifada, which had broken out at the end of 1987. But since the return of the PLO, and the start of what the Oslo Accords called the Interim Phase, much had changed. Civil affairs were now largely in the hands of the Palestinians themselves and the Israeli military authorities had redeployed, assuming a new role that reduced direct interaction with Palestinian society. Massive international funding poured in, and the rising materialism of a new elite was much in evidence. The spirit of voluntarism was in short supply. The ideals of liberation, both personal and political, seemed further off than ever. But what could be done to stop the erosion of values, Mustafa wondered? And what political role was suitable for someone like him during times as turbulent and unstable as these? We had much to talk about on our walk.

We decided not to start from Ramallah. We got a ride to A'yn Qenya. From the village we were going to walk to Deir Ammar, passing through Janiya and the high village of Ras Karkar. With the exception of the last, which was built on the top of the hill as its name implied (the word *ras* meaning 'head'), Palestinians built their villages to embrace the hills not to ride them. This policy gave them protection from strong winds and severe weather conditions. The Israelis, with an eye on security and military advantage, took the hilltops. This is why the settlements stand out. One can tell, by looking at the hills, a Jewish settlement from a Palestinian village. The houses in the hastily constructed settlements are like a honeycomb, with the buildings marshalled next to each other in a rigid plan, while the unplanned Palestinian villages have developed slowly over a long period of time and blend organically into the land. I knew all this. Still, I was in for a surprise. Over the years I had extensively read and written about the Israeli master plans for the settlements. I knew that Israeli planners worked on strangling our inhabited areas and separating them from each other. Sometimes as I read I felt a shudder of fear about the future: What if these plans were fulfilled right here next to where I lived? What would become of us? But reading is not like seeing. From the distance of Ramallah I could not begin to imagine the extent of the upheaval and havoc that the widespread and accelerated building of settlements now taking place around Ramallah was causing in our hills.

It was a mere seven-minute drive down to A'yn Qenya, where the taxi dropped us. This small village never seemed to grow, despite its proximity to Ramallah. It remained unconnected to the water network. The women and the young continued to make the daily trudge to the spring to fill jerry cans with water, load them on donkeys or swing them on their shoulders, and carry them up to their homes. Around the spring, which has given the town its name, you always saw lines of people waiting their turn to fill up from the nozzle of fresh cool water that on previous walks I had drunk from and washed my face with. But this time we were not stopping at the spring. From the centre of the village, where the taxi dropped us, we walked down to the stream in Wadi Dalb that flowed west. By the edge of the road leading to the valley I could see piles of rubbish discarded by the villagers. There was no garbage collection or any means of disposing of waste here and so it was all thrown out in the open. In the past, before the introduction of synthetic substances like plastic and Styrofoam, nature would take care of the biodegradable refuse; now it piled up, forming unsightly mounds, much of which eventually found its way into the wadi and was carried to other parts of the open fields. As we passed this eyesore I thought that, for walkers like us, the village and the valley are seen as one integral whole, but for those living here only their house and the small area surrounding it were considered their space, to be kept clean.

On the hill west of the village the settlement of Dolev, established some decade and a half earlier, had outstanding views and a better-organized and funded local authority that applied Israeli law. The Jewish settlers had no relationship with their Arab neighbours.

The Israeli authorities had declared the area in which A'yn Qenya lay a mature reserve called *Shemurat Delavim*. It was prohibited to litter such areas. But nothing was done to manage the refuse from the Arab village that was destroying the beautiful valley. Perhaps the Israeli authorities were hoping that the village of A'yn Qenya would somehow vanish.

Dolev was not a dynamic settlement. For a relatively long time, as Jewish settlements go, it had remained confined to the top of the hill. Its population did not exceed 2,500 inhabitants. The hill on which it was established had been forested and the settlers had planted more trees between their houses which made it blend better with its surroundings than other settlements. Had this been the only settlement in the area the matter would not have been too serious. Good neighbourly relations could have developed in time between the two communities. But Dolev was only one in an ambitious master plan that called for clusters of settlements linked by a network of roads, wide and straight, that connected the inhabitants to the coastal plain in the shortest possible time. To realize these plans required extensive reshaping of the hills and more destruction than had ever before been wrought on them.

For many years I had been monitoring the orders issued by the Israeli military government declaring parts of the West Bank nature reserves. The first order, number 554, was issued on 16 July 1974. Since then it had been amended at least twenty times. Wadi Qelt was one of the first such reserves. At first I was pleased that legislation was being introduced to protect these spectacular spots, even if it was coming from the occupier. At last the military were doing something beneficial for the land. It was comforting to know that construction and road building would not be allowed and that the natural flora and fauna would be protected. But my hope that the order was made for our benefit was dashed when another related order was passed in 1996 forbidding entry into the so-called area C by non-Israeli nationals without permission from the military governor. All nature reserves were in area C and so, legally, were now out of reach for us Palestinians.

I was aware before we began that the route Mustafa and I were planning to take was prohibited to us. We did not have permission from the military governor to walk there and if we came upon soldiers we could be arrested. A Jewish settler also has the power to make a citizen's arrest. We had to be careful of both. I was certain that Mustafa, like most Palestinians, was unaware of this prohibition. Before we started our walk I considered telling him but in the end decided against it. One anxious person on this lovely walk was enough.

After crossing the piles of garbage at the top of the hill we walked down through a newly ploughed olive field to the wadi. We found the footpath along the stream and took it. It was such a rare pleasure to walk by water in these dry hills. To our right we could see 'raq Es Sahel, the impressive cliffs popular with rock climbers. We continued to amble along in silence, listening to the gurgling water as it made its slow way between the rocks, when suddenly I heard a ring. I was startled and Mustafa was embarrassed. He reached down and pulled up his trouser leg to reveal a mobile phone, which he had attached to his leg in an effort to conceal it. I had insisted on no phones during our walk. I was annoyed by this disruption but realized I had to accept that my friend could not stay out of contact. He was a politician and the conversation revolved around his party. Even for the few hours of the walk he could not stay away from it.

The valley where we walked was relatively wide, a swathe of green cutting through the dry hills. It stretched all the way to Ramallah and was the wadi that Abu Ameen would use to get to his *qasr* in Harrasha. Nearby was an excellent path going north, connecting A'yn Qenya with the villages of Birzeit, Kober and Mizr'a Qiblieh. They lay beyond the two escarpments of 'raq El Khafs and 'raq El Khanouq which were visible to us as we walked. To the south stood Dolev and beyond it the smaller hamlets that were scattered between the hills all the way to the coastal plain and eventually the Mediterranean Sea. The field to our right as we strolled by the stream was cultivated with olives. It was partially shaded by the hill on which Dolev stood. The newly ploughed ground between the olive trees was dappled with spots of shade and light where the sun shown through the branches.

The settlers in Dolev must be unused to seeing walkers strolling down the wadi. Village people do not take walks for pleasure, just as leisure swimming was not common in poor communities living by the sea, simply because there was no time for leisure. I knew there were armed guards around the settlement and wondered who they'd think we were if they happened to look down. I hoped they would not shoot at us or come down and arrest us.

Now our path crossed the wadi. We were able to ford the stream by stepping on wet rocks, catching up with the path on the other side of the narrow valley. The path continued in a north-westerly easy climb beyond the ploughed field into other fields planted with olives that had not been pruned, forcing us to stoop and push our way through their woody branches. Perhaps it was safer to be in this field, concealed by the trees from the watchful eyes of the settlement guards. The unploughed earth here had an abundance of wild flowers mottled with the shadows of the clouds. We stepped back when we saw a number of partridges scurrying away from us on their short legs, until they found a way of flying out of the intertwined branches to feed on seeds in other fields.

Not far from where we walked we saw two young men on horseback riding through the hills. It was a beautiful sight. We followed them with our eyes and saw that they stopped just below the hill where Dolev stood, at a stable belonging to the settlement. The track we were following diverged from the wadi that circled the Dolev hill and led to what appeared to be a country club where Israelis and tourists could come to enjoy our lovely hills.

As we neared the top of the hill the clods of soil began to feel wet even though there was no spring nearby and it hadn't rained. We soon realized that we had walked into the open sewers of the Jewish settlement of Talmon to the north. This settlement might have had a rubbish collection system but it did not have one for treating sewage, which was just disposed of down the valley into land owned by Palestinian farmers. We tried to step lightly so as not to drown our shoes in the settlers' shit. As we trudged through the soggy ground we met two boys who showed us the way out of the bog. We noticed they were taking us away from the paved road and told them that was where we were headed.

'It's too dangerous,' they said.

We asked them why.

'The settlers,' they said. 'If you're walking and they

drive by they swerve and hit you. They ran over Mazen. And if an army jeep comes they shoot. No one uses the road.'

We insisted and they reluctantly came along. I thought they might be exaggerating the danger as boys are wont to do, but I could tell by the way they behaved that using the road leading to their village was to them an adventure. I noticed that they made sure they were flanked by us and stayed on the side of the road, pricking their ears to hear if a settler car or an army jeep was approaching, presumably so that they could run back to the hills. All along the way they rambled nervously, going from one terrifying tale to another about what the settlers had done.

'Abu Nabeel has been unable to get to his olives over there,' the younger one said, pointing to a field which we had just crossed. 'He has been unable to plough. Every time he tried the settlers shot at him and drove him and his sons away.'

I did not notice any Palestinian cars passing by. I thought this was curious.

'Do the people in Janiya ever drive along this road?' I asked.

'They can't,' the older boy told me. 'The entrance to the village is blocked.'

When we got to the road leading to the village we could see the concrete blocks the army had placed across the entrance, a barrier which no one was allowed to remove. I wondered whether the villagers would be allowed to ride a mule or a horse on the road, if they happened to own one. I suspected not.

From the point of view of the settlers these measures were necessary to protect them from stone throwers. So convinced were they of their moral superiority that they proceeded to use their practical immunity from prosecution to intimidate their neighbours. Some used their firearms to shoot and kill Palestinians in cold blood. From as early as 1982 incidents of settler violence were documented by Al Haq and others. But Israeli prosecutors rarely took action against the settlers, much as human rights groups, Israeli and Palestinian, lobbied for this.

Janiya was a larger and richer village than A'yn Qenya. A substantial number of its inhabitants had emigrated to the United States, where they had done well and were sending remittances to the village to help out their relatives. We walked up the asphalted road leading to the centre and, after asking around, were directed to the path that led to the next wadi. Before us spread the gorgeous Wadi El Ghadeer ('the brook'), which was wider and much more lush than Wadi Dalb. Again, as in A'yn Qenya, we came upon piles of garbage at the edge of the village. The walk down was a steeper incline than any we had taken so far and it led to grassy fields. As we walked down we could see and hear bulldozers turning the ground northeast of the village as they broke the bedrock to prepare the foundations for the new settlements of Talmon Beth, Harasha and Horesh Yaron, next to the already existing Talmon. I tried hard to block out the sound but it was impossible.

It was curious that we did not find any villagers working on their land here. Traditionally these were agricultural villages. Within a few decades the inhabitants have been intimidated, their life made unsafe and many of their fields expropriated, and they have been turned into construction workers building the settlements which stood on land that once had belonged to them. These were

the beginnings of new times, a new relationship to the
land and the destruction of the hills as I knew them.

When we got to the wadi our path turned northward
and we were now too low to be able to see the construction work taking place above us on the hills to the east.
We were walking on a lush green swell cultivated with
chickpeas when we came upon an adobe structure. It
was freshly painted in white and stood out starkly from
the sea of green. It was the *maqam* of Nabi Aneer. The
maqamat (plural) are tombs of revered sheikhs (elders)
or local saints. Usually a small domed structure would
be built around the tomb, where locals could go to pray
and meditate. Mustafa and I spoke in hushed voices as we
approached. When we reached the door, we looked in but
it was dark inside. When our eyes adjusted we could see
a bearded man sitting in total silence. We quickly pulled
ourselves away for we did not want to disturb him. He
had left his shoes outside and was squatting beneath the
dome, meditating.

We moved away, walking in silence along the path
that now began to climb southward towards the high
village of Ras Karkar, one of twenty-odd throne villages in
Palestine. These were the seats of rural nobility who, with
the weakening of the centralized Ottoman authority,
collected taxes on its behalf and achieved great political
and socio-economic power in their local areas. Those who
failed to pay had their land expropriated. The village was
originally called Janiet Sheikh Sam'an after the sheikh
who governed it. He had built a citadel in the village and
lived in it. During the First World War the village head
sided with the Ottomans. After they began their rule over
Palestine the British punished him by changing the name
of the village from Janiet Shiekh Sam'an to its original

name of Ras Karkar. The Arabic word *ras* means head and *karkar* is a skua. But since these birds are not indigenous to the area it is more likely that the British were thinking of the other meaning of the word, which is to burst out in laughter.

The green grass on both sides of the path was so high it dwarfed us as we walked west, far away from any village or settlement. We were surrounded by open fields in hills that, except for the few narrow roads built long ago, must have remained unchanged since biblical times. For a long time my enjoyment of these hills has been impaired by a preoccupation with the changes in land law relating to them. But such man-made constructs can be diminished if looked at in a particular way. Viewed from the perspective of the land they hardly count. A road makes a scar in the hills but over time that scar heals and becomes absorbed and incorporated. Stones are gathered to build houses but then they crumble and return to the land, however large and formidable they might once have been. Monumental Crusader castles in a dilapidated state dot the land, as do the ruins of other empires that have prevailed in this region. Empires and conquerors come and go but the land remains. As these thoughts crossed my mind, I could not help but wonder whether this long-term perspective was simply another justification for having curtailed my activism, or a reasonable defence against Israel's positing of these changes as permanent and incapable of ever being altered. I realized that the stronger the attempt at impressing me with their permanence, the more my mind sought confirmation of their transience.

Thinking in the long term made it possible for me to separate 'the present' from the rest of time and thereby realize that what Palestine and Israel are now would not necessarily be for ever. I was here on earth for a relatively short period and after that time passed, life would go on without my points of view, biases and fears.

In 'Carmel Point' the poet Robinson Jeffers asks whether nature cares when 'the spoiler has come' and answers:

> Not faintly. It has all time. It knows the people are a
> tide
> That swells and in time will ebb, and all
> Their works dissolve. Meanwhile the image of the
> pristine beauty
> Lives in the very grain of the granite,
> Safe as the endless ocean that climbs our cliff – as for
> us:
> We must uncenter our minds from ourselves;
> We must unhumanize our views a little, and become
> confident
> As the rock and ocean that we were made from.

Mustafa has known me for a long time and must have noticed how this line of thinking had changed me. At one point in the course of our walk he turned to me and asked: 'Tell me, how did you get over your anger?'

I was surprised by the question. I had not realized that I was coming across as a less angry man. At first I did not know how to answer and merely replied: 'By accepting the fact of our surrender and moving on.'

Almost immediately after saying this I was aware that I had left out the most important factor. More than anything else it was writing that was helping me overcome the anger that burns in the heart of most Palestinians. In my memoir, *Strangers in the House,* I had written about the experience of my parents and grandparents in the *Nakbeh* of 1948. Through feeling and expressing their pain, as well as my own, over that wrenching past I was able to liberate myself from the yoke of something that had so dominated my imagination that I found it difficult to go beyond it. My own experiences were dwarfed by the enormity of what had happened before I was born. It was also true that since I had redirected my energies from activism to writing I found I was more in my element. I had never been entirely comfortable as a political activist. Conditions had imposed that role on me.

'You think the deal was that bad?' Mustafa asked.

'This is not the first time we have arrived at defeat that was trumpeted by the leadership as a victory,' I replied. 'Our history is rich with similar instances. The price of living a lie is too high for me. I'd rather face facts and take stock. Israel has won this round. It will take many years to undo the harm of Oslo. We might be able to gain valuable time if we face the fact of our defeat.'

'I'm under strong pressure from my party to accept an invitation to join the government. You cannot begin to imagine how insistent they are. They say it is the only game in town. I agree with you in thinking it is doomed but there are huge rewards from joining – high governmental positions, money, power. It's like holding back the trophy which everyone can see and wants to get at. I've tried. I did everything I could to tell them what I thought of the Agreement and the Authority. It will destroy our future chances if we go after easy gains. I am certain of it. What I'm less sure of is the alternative. What role could we play if we are not in government?'

'The same role you've always played, as opposition.'

'But we did this when the occupation exercised all civilian powers.'

'You don't have to relate to the Palestinian Authority as the enemy. What I'm suggesting is that you see it as a passing phenomenon and prepare for the next stage.'

'And what do you think that would be?'

'The continuation of the struggle. The Agreement was an act of surrender. In its wake there is more heightened settlement activity than before. The Israeli side's understanding is that they have shared the West Bank, giving us areas A and B and leaving C for themselves. This is why they have declared it a closed military zone and are proceeding to fill it up with settlements.'

'Area C is closed? I didn't know this.'

'It's been closed by military order since 1996.'

'Then we are here illegally.'

'Absolutely.'

'And our Authority is silent. They've done nothing to challenge Israel over this, as if the issue doesn't concern them.'

'They probably don't know about it.'

'But they should. Aren't they, the government, responsible? How can they not know?'

We were in agreement that the most important work that could now be done was the empowering of civil society. This sector, Mustafa thought, had a strong role to play in countering the excesses and mistakes our new and inexperienced government would be making. He was an astute enough politician to know that he could not criticize the Oslo Agreement while in government. To join would be a trap, like selling his voice.

'I've already started a campaign,' Mustafa told me, 'against the proposed law on Non-Governmental

Organizations. The draft the government prepared imposes all sorts of restrictions on this sector. If it passes as proposed it would make matters much worse for us, worse even than it was under full Israeli rule. They are trying to do this so that they have a free hand politically. We have to be there to put the brakes on.'

Mustafa always knew what he wanted; I only supplied him with the legal arguments that confirmed his political hunches.

We had now circled the attractive village whose houses straddled the peaked *ras* and proceeded to walk westward under the full glare of the sun. Mustafa began to tell me about his experience at the Allenby Bridge between the West Bank and Jordan during his last return from a trip abroad. He thought it illustrated what I had just been saying:

'When I arrived I gave the Palestinian official at the border my travel documents. He passed them on immediately, without even checking them, to the Israeli in a booth right behind him. I couldn't help noticing that the paint over the glass that separated the two officials, which is supposed to hide the Israeli, had faded. This, I thought, was symbolic of the whole Oslo deal,' Mustafa chuckled. 'I could see through the screen, the deception that is the Oslo Agreement. The Palestinian flag, which the Palestinian negotiators wasted many sessions fighting for, was nowhere in sight. It had been removed. The Israeli exercise of sovereignty over the border was absolute. Their official behind the glass with the faded paint apparently wanted to see me. This was communicated to me by the hapless Palestinian official. I simply refused to go. I told him: "Aren't you ashamed of yourself, obeying the orders of the Israeli? So far I have been treated royally and now have to submit to the Israeli *mukhabart* [security service]? I refuse to go. You can do what you like with me."

'I was kept there until midnight when it was finally agreed that the Israeli would come out of his box and stand in a line with the Palestinian officials and that they would all shake my hand and then the Israeli would hand me my passport. This way the Israeli could assert his presence and make it clear that he was the one with real power.

'I asked the Palestinian officers at the bridge how they could tolerate this stupid charade. They agreed that the deal that had been negotiated was a bad one but they could do nothing about it. I said we should not be taking this lying down. I was delayed for many hours at the bridge but in the end I made my point. If everyone resisted these practices we would get somewhere. After they gave me back my passport, I refused to shake the hand of the Israeli official. Instead I told him: "I will be sending you my picture." "Why?" the Israeli asked. "To hang it on the wall of your cubicle so that you will see me constantly," I said. "Weren't you anxious to see me?"'

We continued our walk westward below the village and down to Wadi El Shoak ('the thistles'). Again we could hear earth-moving equipment working above us and realized that they were opening a new road through the hills that would connect the settlement of Talmon in the east and Na'ale to the north-west with the urban settlements of Modi'in Illit and Matityahu that straddle the green line, a straight four-lane highway in these undulating hills.

When we climbed up again the whole scene of the new construction lay bare before our eyes. There was so much upheaval, it was as though the entire earth was being re-shuffled. Developers were levelling hills, destroying the terracing and excavating large boulders from the ground for service in retaining walls. Israeli settlements no longer consisted of modest enclaves planted in our midst that could be reversed. Enormous changes were taking place that it was hard not to see as permanent. It was as though the tectonic movements that had occurred over thousands of years were now happening in a matter of months, entirely re-drawing the map. The Palestine I knew, the land I had thought of as mine, was quickly being transformed before my eyes.

Several hills north of where we walked was the settlement of Halamish, close to Deir Ghassaneh, the village where Mustafa's family originated. During the war of 1967 his father sent him and his siblings to the village, thinking it would be safer there than in Ramallah. On their way back from the village Mustafa met his first Israeli.

'I will never forget it,' he told me. 'I remember every detail. My father had sent us with my mother to Deir Ghassaneh. I was still very young, fourteen years or so. When the Israeli army arrived the people thought they were Nasser's Egyptian soldiers. We were going back home when they stopped us and asked to see identification. I lost my innocence that day. I realized that the faith we had put in Nasser was misplaced. The man could not save us and I felt a strong responsibility on my shoulders. I have to work hard now, I thought, because our fate rests with us. When Nasser tried to resign the elders were angry with him. They were spiteful. My own reaction was different. I thought the man could not do it. It was not within his capabilities. This did not make me feel any malice towards him.'

I realized how similar Mustafa's reactions were to my father's. Both men had applied all their energy to the national cause. They only came to believe in a peaceful negotiated settlement to the conflict after full consideration of other options. Despite their age difference, the 1967 war was a turning point for both of them. After my father proposed his peaceful resolution to the conflict, he was attacked by the extremists on both sides whose politics have only brought us disaster. Likewise those who found fault in Mustafa's strategy were also numerous. In a society as small as this, envy also plays a role. A local leader can get nowhere armed only with good intentions and political acumen. As my father realized late in his life money played a big role in moving people, as it does everywhere in the world.

Throughout our walk in these hills we had not come across a single soldier or settler and yet we felt their presence all around us as they continued to build new settlements, enlarge existing ones and connect them with roads. This did not bode well for the future. As we descended further down into the valley, the hills muffled the sound and we could pretend once again that this land would remain ours, a place where we could walk in peace and silence, undisturbed.

We now got to Wadi El Nada ('the dew'), which we found awash with yellow mustard seed and the blue bugloss. But the dominant colour in the flat wide valley below Deir Ammar was the bright red of vast flocks of poppies. There were a few clouds in the sky that filtered the sun, making the wide wadi look even more striking. When the sun emerged from behind the clouds, the intensity of colour strengthened. The grass became radiant and when it swayed with the light wind different shades of green were exposed. We decided to sit at the edge of this valley before we started our climb up to Deir Ammar, our final destination.

As we climbed we could see the verdant fields with patches of rocks in between, little grey islands bathed on all sides by the yellow of the broom rising in spiky leaves above the grass. But as we got close to the village we were bombarded with the putrid smell of an animal carcass, so strong we had to hold our noses and run away as fast as we could. When we got up the hill we stopped and looked down at the valley from a distance, and were only then aware of a group of young boys who had gathered around us, curious about who these two middle-aged men racing up the hill might be. The clouds had cleared, and everything shone in the bright clear light. Such beautiful fields, such a beautiful, spoiled country!

Mustafa was known in Deir Ammar. The village had a refugee camp, established in 1949 on village land and run by the United Nations Relief and Works Agency (UNRWA), where the Palestinians whom Israel expelled from the border villages in 1948 settled. In return the UN Agency provided non-refugees in the village with services. Mustafa had come with others from the Medical Relief Organization that he ran to provide free medical services to the villagers during the numerous sieges Israel imposed on the village during the first Intifada.

By the end of our walk I had realized how necessary it was to go beyond mere recognition of our desperate political state. I had been dwelling too much on the past, indulging in self-flagellation over what I assessed was our defeat, which I was perhaps all too eager to recognize. I was grateful to Mustafa for encouraging me to start thinking about what could be done rather than succumbing to despair. I tried to remind myself that I should see the past in a more positive light. I was privileged to have had the opportunity of participating in the public struggle. This and only this was my reward. I had no right to make further claims to the fruits of my labour.

❧

Our assessment of the Oslo Accords has been proven correct. The agreement with Israel proved to be a false start, with disastrous consequences for the Palestinian struggle to end the occupation and achieve statehood. Politically Mustafa had done well not to join the newly established Palestinian Authority. He left the People's Party where for many years he had served as a high-ranking member. He formed his own party and after the death of Yasser Arafat in 2005 ran for head of the Palestinian Authority. He did well, managing to win about a quarter of the vote. For a number of years he served as a member of the Palestinian Legislative Council and became a cabinet minister in the unity government established in March 2007.

I continue to be peripherally involved in public matters helping Mustafa, as a fellow traveller, where and when I can. But most of my attention remains focused on my writing. My house continues to be the sanctuary I had hoped it would be, where Penny and I can retreat, living as quiet a life as is possible in this war-torn land.

But the country was not moving towards peace. The suffocating closure of the West Bank by the Israeli army and the continuation of intensive settlement construction throughout the land were creating tremendous pressure on the period of calm that the Oslo Agreement, with all its faults, had ushered in.

During earlier geological eras the pressure on the land

mounted and mounted until it could bear no more and cracked, forming the Great Rift Valley. Only peace could circumvent a similar rupture between the two people living on the same land. But the Israeli government was unwilling to leave the land or its people in peace.

As Mustafa and I witnessed during our walk in the hills, our land was being transformed before our eyes, and a new map was being drawn. We were not supposed to look, only to blindly believe in the hollow language of peace proclaimed by Israeli leaders, a peace that amounted to mere words, rhetoric that meant nothing.

But an entire nation cannot indulge for long in voluntary blindness. Predictably another cycle of violence soon began, this time a more violent Intifada than the first, one that threatened to bring about the ultimate cleavage between the two peoples, one that would be unbridgeable.

6

AN IMAGINED *SARHA*

Wadi Dalb

Much has happened since the last walk described above. My hope that I would find refuge in my stone house was dispelled in the spring of 2002, when the Israeli army invaded Ramallah, entered my home and broke the sense of sanctuary I had ascribed to it. The ostensible reason given by Israel for invading West Bank cities was to defend the country. Such was the power of ideology that in the eyes of most Israelis, 'Israel' had come to mean 'the Greater Land of Israel', including most of the settlements. In fact maps used in Israeli school books had done away with the pre-1967 borders between Israel and the Occupied Territories. To defend their 'country' also meant to defend the settlements in the Occupied Territories. In its decisions the Israeli High Court confirmed this. The settlers, it ruled, had a basic right to be protected by the state. The fact that they were on illegally acquired land made no difference.

When the Israeli Prime Minister, Ehud Olmert, formulated his ill-fated plan in 2006 to annex the Jewish settlements in the occupied West Bank to Israel, he called it the Convergence Plan. The old Israel of the pre-1967 borders was to converge with the new Israel in the occupied West Bank to form 'Greater Israel'. Thirteen years after Israel had committed itself under the Oslo Agreement to negotiating with its Palestinian neighbours the fate of the Jewish settlements during final status talks, the government announced that it was planning to determine their status unilaterally by annexing most of them to Israel and redrawing the borders of the state without further negotiations. After the annexation the Palestinians would be left with scattered, non-contiguous areas of land that could not possibly constitute the basis of a viable state. So powerful had Israel become, and such was the unlimited support it was getting from the United States and its British ally, that it felt it could renege on earlier commitments to the Palestinians with total impunity.

A number of these settlements had been established after commando operations against Israel by Palestinian resistance fighters, with the Israeli government claiming that their establishment was 'the proper Zionist response'. Over the years the Zionist ideology never evolved to the point of believing that the only policy which would ensure its long-term survival would be to seek peace with its Arab neighbours and integrate in the region, rather than proceed to antagonize further the Palestinians by taking more of their land and planting foreign enclaves within their territory. Just as Israel remained in a state of enmity with the people and states around it, so the settlers were living in total isolation from the indigenous Palestinian inhabitants of the land. Israeli leaders were fond of repeating that they wanted to 'sear into our consciousness' the Jewish presence in our land. In other words to make us surrender our rights to it.

The invasion of Ramallah was followed by drastic

measures that continued long after the army withdrew. Using security as a justification, entrances to all the cities and hundreds of villages were closed. Use of most roads in the West Bank was prohibited to Palestinians, forcing us to use unpaved roads that had to be travelled in secret, mere tracks that went over rocks and took dangerous bends, damaging the cars that travelled them.

The large number of checkpoints and obstacles placed by the Israeli army on West Bank roads complicated our lives immeasurably. Even after the bombing in Israel had stopped, they increased in number from 376 in August 2005 to 528 by October 2006. We now moved in our own country surreptitiously, like unwanted strangers, constantly harassed, never feeling safe. We had become temporary residents of Greater Israel, living on Israel's sufferance, subject to the most abusive treatment at the hands of its young male and female soldiers controlling the checkpoints, deciding on a whim whether to keep us waiting for hours or allowing us passage. But worse than all this was that nagging feeling that our days in Palestine were numbered and one day we were going to be victims of another mass expulsion.

The residents of Ramallah, the centre of the Palestinian Authority, did not escape the constraints of the ghetto life experienced in other West Bank cities. All entrances to the city were controlled by the Israeli army. At the Beitunia exit south-west of Ramallah on the road leading to Beit 'Ur, where Albina's land is situated, a prison that began as a temporary tent facility for incarcerating juvenile offenders had now become a permanent, ever-expanding fortress, with watchtowers and high walls topped by barbed wire where the Israeli military court was convened. A highway cut through the low hills going from east to west, restricting Ramallah's expansion in that direction. It was reserved for the use of Jewish settlers travelling from Jerusalem and the settlements around its north-western borders to Tel Aviv and the coastal plain. Passage through this exit was prohibited to Palestinians.

Those settlements around Ramallah that existed at the time of the Oslo Accords had been enlarged and more than ten new ones added, some on land that even the discriminatory Israeli legal system recognized as Palestinian. One of these, in the north-west of Ramallah, bore a similar sounding name to Abu Ameen's summer farm, Harrasha. When I look at night from the roof of my house at the horizon I can see the yellow lights of these illegal outposts creating an illuminated noose around the city.

But the most destructive development, which boded only misery and spelled continued conflict for the future, was the wall being constructed by Israel. This stretched in a jagged course that was determined not only by Israeli military considerations but also by the special interests of settlers and land mafia lords, slicing through the hills, destroying their natural shape, gulping large swathes of Palestinian land. Only in part did it follow the 1967 armistice's internationally recognized border between Israel and the Palestinian territories, which has now been deleted from official Israeli maps of the area. The 'settlement blocs' Israel planned to annex, which thrust like daggers into the Palestinian land, were now sheathed by the wall.

Still, I was determined that none of this was going to prevent me from taking more walks in the hills. Not the military orders closing most of the West Bank, not the checkpoints and roadblocks, and not the Jewish settlements. Weather-wise that spring of 2006 was one of the best for many years. The rain had been plentiful but also well distributed. It even continued to rain through April, giving vital sustenance to the wild flowers that by the end of the month usually begin to shrivel and die. I could not let this season pass without a walk.

A slight damper on my audacity was my determination not to repeat a terrifying experience I had a few months earlier when, driving back from the Jordan valley, I got lost. I must have taken a wrong turn and found myself in the midst of new settlements and industrial zones, vast open spaces that made me wonder what country I was in. I told myself not to panic and that if I continued driving westward I must eventually emerge in an area I would recognize. But the further I drove the more lost I became. All the signposts pointed to Jewish settlements. I could find none of the features that used to guide me on my way: that beautiful cluster of boulders, those cliffs just after the bend that dips into the valley and up again onto the road with the attractive village to the right. 'Where am I?' I kept asking myself. At first I tried to pretend that it was just a game. I had enough petrol in my car and eventually I would surely be able to find my way out of this maze. But as time passed and I was not seeing anywhere I recognized, panic struck. As a child I had a recurring nightmare in which I found myself in a strange place unable to find my way home. I would try to shout for help only to realize that I had no voice. This felt like a similar situation. I began to sweat. Where was I? How would I ever get out of this? It began to get dark and with the twilight the land became even more unfamiliar. My driving was getting reckless. I was not stopping at crossroads. Circling around without any notion of where I was going had induced a mental trance.

There were no other cars on these roads. I seemed to be the sole traveller in this never-never land, experiencing this waking nightmare entirely alone. 'Perhaps I should stop and collect myself,' I told myself. But how would this help? Penny always advises me to take a deep breath when I'm caught in such situations. But this was different. I did not know where to begin to extricate myself from the mess I had got myself in. My heart began to beat fast. I felt I had finally been ensnared in the labyrinth of settlements I had long been pursuing and would never be allowed to escape. After my petrol ran out I would have to remain here until someone came to save me. But who other than armed settlers roamed this new world in the midst of my old familiar surroundings? I was utterly exhausted when, in the end, I finally managed to find a way out. How I did so, I will never know.

I suspected that with the construction of all the new settlements and the roads connecting them, I might easily get lost again. I decided to be extra cautious and choose my path with the utmost care.

I surveyed my prospects. I could not go to A'yn Qenya through the Abu Ameen track because much of it had been destroyed by new buildings in the course of Ramallah's expansion to the north-west. Added to this was the fact that the Jewish settlers from Dolev and Beit Eil had raised money to build a bypass road through our hills and valleys, going over private Palestinian lands to connect their two settlements. This badly designed private road caused much damage to the hills and obstructed the passage of the water through the wadi. It also destroyed a number of the springs and many unique rock formations, amongst them a beautiful cliff which in spring was studded with cyclamens that I often stopped to admire.

As to the valley to the south where I found the dinosaur footprints, it was now used for target practice by members of the Palestinian security forces. At night one could hear the staccato dribble of their guns. Its access to A'yn Qenya was also blocked by the army post on the hillock owned by the Rabah family half a kilometre down from the Yad Yair military outpost.

So I decided to consult a map of the hills. I had to. It was not a practice I would have chosen for it implied submission to others, the makers of the maps, with their ideological biases. I would much rather have exercised the freedom of going by the map inside my head, sign-posted by historical memories and references: this area where Abu Ameen has his *qasr*, that rock where Jonathan and I stopped and had a long talk. That hill over which Penny and I had a memorable walk. But I had no choice. To find a track I could take that was without settlers or practice shooters or army posts or settler bypass roads had become a real challenge.

I was finally able to work out a route. I would take a taxi and travel north towards Birzeit through area B, which Palestinians could still enter without a permit from the Israeli army. Just before reaching the university campus I would ask the taxi to take a left turn and travel east to the village of Mizra'a Qibliya. There he would drop me. I still had to risk going into area C but I had found a path that avoided army posts, bypasses, and Jewish settlements. I would walk down in a south-westerly direction to avoid the settlement of Talmon and its new daughter settlements: Harasha, Horesh Yaron, Nahlei Tal and Zayit Ra'anan. Then down to the A'yn Qenya spring. Walk in a northerly direction in the valley, then circle back to Ramallah avoiding Yad Yair and the other army post on Jabal Kwa'a.

When we reached Mizra'a I asked the driver to take me up the hill.

'To Harrasha?' he asked.

'Yes,' I replied, my heart pounding at hearing the name. I was driven up a steep hill to where there was a copse of pine trees.

'Here it is,' the driver said. 'Is this where you want to be dropped?' I could tell he was wondering what business I could possibly have there.

I found myself all alone in a land that might have once resembled Abu Ameen's. A green pine stood with a spring nearby high up on the hill next to a cultivated orchard. My spirits revived. I felt empowered by the memory of Abu Ameen and his much different times. I did not care what happened to me, I was going to enjoy my walk in the hills. I continued along the track, which I easily found, going south and climbing still higher until I got to 'raq El Khanouq, the escarpment overlooking Wadi Dalb. It was too high and vertiginous for me to descend. Instead I continued walking northwards until I got to the gully and found a track formed by the passage of rainwater streaming down the valley in winter, a steep track but made gorgeous by the view it offered of the valley below with its wide swathe of green and the water flowing in its midst shimmering in the mid-morning light. I could not get over how unusual it was to see a green valley with a brook in these dry hills. My heart leapt. I almost ran down the path but thought better of it and, out of kindness to my knees, I slowed down. I felt secure enough on this track and intended to continue on it until I got to the cultivated fields south-east of A'yn Qenya.

Just as I reached the water I realized that someone else was already there. I noticed him from the corner of my eye. I did not look directly at him. I did not want to allow him to disturb my peace. But I knew he was there and that he was an Israeli settler.

It was then that I noticed a strong, unusual smell. I realized it was that of hashish mixed with another more potent substance which I could not identify. When I arrived, the settler was busy preparing his *nergila* (water pipe or hubble-bubble), on a flat rock right next to the stream. He was surprised by my unexpected entry into his private little enclave and stopped what he was doing. He must have realized that I was aware of his illicit activity. He could not be immediately certain who I was: perhaps an Israeli, a man of the law, someone who could arrest him for smoking the forbidden weed. But of course *he* had the authority; *he* was the law. He also had a gun. And a settler can shoot at a Palestinian with impunity.

I took a careful look at his face. It was narrow with a prominent nose and kind, intelligent eyes. He had long straight brown hair that reached down to his shoulders falling on both sides of his head like a scarf. He was clearly an Israeli settler, as I had assumed from the start. I didn't want to judge him. I wanted to be on my way. Without uttering a word I concentrated on choosing the best stepping stones to ford the brook. I almost got to the other side when I heard him call, in Hebrew:

'Your hat. You've dropped your hat.'

He had a soft, kind voice. Still, I was surprised to be accosted by the settler. I had somehow not expected it, and was hoping to just slip by, unseen, unseeing, each to his own. But this was not to be. Not any more, not in the Palestinian hills in the spring of 2006.

My hat was going downstream, quickly. I crouched to

get it but couldn't. I saw it floating and bobbing over the rocks. The Israeli rushed after it. He was younger and more nimble than me. He caught it. He stood there holding my dripping hat for me. My gaze wandered from him to the rock where he had balanced his *nergila* and where his gun also rested. His eyes followed mine and I saw him stiffen, evidently trying to decide between running to the gun and giving me my hat. I didn't move. I was curious which way he would go. He could not be sure whether I was Palestinian or Israeli. Now using English I said:

'Your gun is out of place, leaning against that rock. Don't you think?'

He didn't speak. Perhaps he didn't understand my English. I rephrased what I said:

'This beautiful day and the gun don't go together.'

After a brief silence he spoke. He was almost apologetic, which is most untypical of an Israeli. He said:

'I know but I have to.'

'Where did you come from?'

'Up there.'

'Dolev?'

'Yes.'

'You live there?'

'Yes.'

Looking at the *nergila* I asked rather pointedly: 'Do you come here often?' I was wondering whether he often ran away from home to smoke his dope in private. Our hills now served as refuge for young Israeli settlers indulging in illicit practices.

'It's my favourite spot,' the settler answered.

Of course, I thought. A perfect hideout. I could tell the young man wanted me gone so that he could get on with his preparations for the smoke.

'Aren't you afraid of being here alone?'

'Afraid? Why should I be? I've done no evil to anyone.'

Done no evil, I thought, after all the land he and his people have stolen, after destroying our life for so long.

'Why then carry a gun?'

'I'm supposed to.'

'How convenient for you to live so close to this valley. You just walk down the hill and you're here.'

'I come here to be alone,' the settler said pointedly.

I caught the innuendo but I was not going to go away and leave him now without trying to find out a few things about this unwelcome neighbour of mine.

'Were you born in Dolev?'

'No, but my parents moved here when I was five.'

'When was that?'

'Nineteen eighty-six.'

'You're still doing army duty?'

'I finished. I'm a fireman.'

'You can't have too many fires in Dolev. It's a small community.'

'I work at the Lod Industrial Park. What about you? Where do you come from?'

I thought of giving him the nondescript answer Rema gave the settlers in Wadi Qelt: 'From here,' but decided to tell him the truth. 'Ramallah,' I answered.

'I suspected you were an Arab but was not sure. Arabs don't walk.'

'How do you know that? Are you acquainted with many Arabs?'

'No. None at all.'

'Then how did you come upon that conclusion?'

'Just from watching the village people nearby. I never see them taking walks or sitting by the water.'

'Perhaps because they're afraid?'

'Why should they be afraid?'

'Because of you.'

'Of me?'

'Yes. Aren't you carrying a gun?'

'I wish I wasn't. It's heavy and it's a burden. But as I said I have to.'

I couldn't help saying: 'I suppose you do' in a heavily sarcastic voice though I regretted doing so almost immediately. I was inviting a fight when I had no stomach or inclination to get into one.

'What do you mean?' the settler snapped.

'To protect the land you've taken from us,' I said in a matter-of-fact way, resigned to what was coming.

'We didn't take anyone's land. Dolev is built entirely on public land.'

'Assuming it is why should you be the only beneficiaries?'

'Because it was promised to us. All of Eretz Israel is ours.'

'And where do you propose we live?'

'You have your place; we have ours.'

'But you're constantly expanding and taking more land. There's hardly any left to build our state.'

'Why do you need another state? You already have twenty-one Arab states. We've only got one.'

I found myself wanting to go. Run away. Get on with my walk. I didn't want to hear more. What had I got myself into? This young man had internalized the official propaganda and was just parroting it. Why should I spoil my walk by listening to such annoying nonsense?

'Can't you think for yourself?' I blurted, reprimanding this youngster despite my earlier resolution not to get into a fight with him. 'Can you only repeat what you've been told?'

He looked at me with an expression of shock and defiance. He was not going to take this. Good, I thought, perhaps now I will get some real emotions and honest thought.

'Did you know that this land you're on has been declared a nature reserve? We are protecting this spot. Except for us it would have been ruined. As a walker you should appreciate this.'

I couldn't believe it. I said: '*You're* protecting *our* land? After all the damage your bulldozers have done digging highways in these hills, pouring concrete to build settlements, you claim to be preserving this land?'

'No one is allowed to build here any more. Or destroy the paths or pick wild flowers. Without these regulations this beautiful spot would be ruined.'

'Let me tell you how things looked when this was truly a nature park. Before you came and spoiled it all. You could not see any new buildings, you did not hear any traffic. All you saw were deer leaping up the terraced hills, wild rabbits, foxes, jackals and carpets of flowers. Then it was a park. Preserved in more or less the same state it had been in for hundreds of years.'

'Nothing can remain untouched for hundreds of years. Progress is inevitable. You would have done the same as we are doing. Only you lacked the material and technical resources to connect these distant areas to power and service them with water and electricity. Look at the villagers here, your fellow Arabs. They still have to fetch their water from the spring. I see them trudging every morning with their heavy buckets. It must be a hell of a life without running water. And look at the areas where your people come for picnics further upstream. They are rubbish dumps full of plastic bags and disposable plates and cups and chicken bones left from their barbecues. You lack the know-how and the discipline. Leave planning and law enforcement to us. We have built many towns and cities out of wild empty areas. Tel Aviv was built on sand dunes and look how vibrant it is today. The same will happen here.'

'God forbid.'

'I love these hills no less than you. I was raised here. The sights and smells of this land are a sacred part of me. I am not happy anywhere else. Every time I leave I cannot wait to get back. This is my home.'

'What do you call this wadi ?'

'Wadi Dolev.'

'And the spring?'

'A'yn Dolev.'

'After the plane tree. You pronounce it Dolev, we say Dalb.'

'Isn't it glorious in spring?'

'This one in particular.'

'Yes. There was more water this year than ever.'

'So unusual for this part of the country.'

'It's very peaceful here.'

'This too is unusual.'

'Where're you heading?'

'No particular place. I came to see what is happening to the valley. It's been a while since I walked.'

'I too love walking. I do a lot of it around these hills.'

I held my breath. I wanted to blurt out all the curses I had ever learned: You ... you ... who've taken my land and now walk it as master, leaving me to walk as a criminal on a few restricted paths. But this time I held my tongue.

'Would you put out a fire in Ramallah?' I asked.

'You have your own firemen, I suppose.'

'What if they couldn't cope and they called you?'

'Would you guarantee I would not be lynched?'

'We're not exactly savages, as you could find out if you visited. Have you ever been to Ramallah? It's just a few minutes away by car.'

'No, not as an adult.'

'As a child?'

'Yes. We used to pass through the city to get to our school in Beit Eil. But I don't remember a thing. The only memory I have is of when we were stoned and the fierce, awful face of that Arab who threw the stone at us. All wrapped up except for the eyes. He flung that stone with such anger and hatred. I felt all this in its impact on the glass. Nothing broke. None of us were injured but it destroyed something inside me, perhaps for ever. This was much worse than if we had been physically injured by broken glass. Then I would have healed. I was so afraid. I cried all the way to school. Not because of what my teachers thought, not because of the stone, but because I could not understand why the Arabs hate us so much. When we got to school I asked the teacher why.'

'And what did she answer?'

'Because they are bad people,' she said, 'and they hate Jews. This is why we have to be strong to defend ourselves."

'And you still think this?'

'I have very little to do with Arabs. Now we have our own roads.'

'The valley road?'

'No. We stopped using that one.'

'You dug our hills for nothing.'

'Building roads is progress, not destruction.'

If only he knew what the presence of that road now used by the army has meant to me. But I wasn't going to tell him. I didn't think he would understand.

'You are aware, I hope, that your presence here means perpetual war.'

'Why?'

'Because you've taken our land and refuse to even recognize the fact.'

'Let's say we give it back: what guarantee would we have that you won't ask to get back Jaffa and Haifa?'

'What about international law?'

'It's for the weak.'

'It's a marker of a better, more civilized world.'

'I went to the army for three years. I will defend everything my family fought for. There was a war and we won. Our presence here is a fact that you will just have to live with. My grandfather died fighting in the war of independence.'

'Independence from whom?'

'The British.'

'But they came to take our country from us and give it to you. Haven't you read the terms of the Mandate?'

'They restricted us. They wouldn't allow the immigrants to come. They wanted us to have only a tiny piece of the country. Israel would not have been a viable state. We had to get rid of them to run our own affairs, to be able to welcome here any Jew from anywhere in the world without anyone telling us not to.'

'Will you pay compensation for the properties you took in '48?'

'If you pay for Jewish losses in Cairo, Baghdad and Yemen.'

'What have we to do with Egypt, with Iraq, with Yemen? Ask them. They are different countries. As far as I'm concerned all people who lost property should be compensated. But you should not link the two cases.'

'They're Arab, aren't they?'

'You're just repeating what you've been told. If you just think about what you're saying you'd realize how ludicrous it is. Let's say we accept that you keep your settlements, would you be willing to be confined to the built-up areas?'

'You want to turn us into ghettoes in our own land. We've been through that in Europe. Never again.'

'Then if you want to expand over the entire land will you allow us to buy or rent in your settlements?'

'No. These are areas for Jews.'

'Let us assume that your settlements are built on what you call public not private land. What people would agree to have areas of their country carved out and given to members of another nation and not even be allowed to share the land?'

'But you're not a nation. You never had your own government.'

'Are you going to repeat the famous position of Golda Meir, that we Palestinians do not exist?'

'No. I didn't say that. I know you exist. I can see you standing before me. And I know you are not Israeli. You exist, sure enough. But you don't have, you never had a national presence in Eretz Israel.'

'And you did?'

'Yes, we had a kingdom right here in Judea.'

'That was more than three thousand years ago.'

'So?'

'So with the exception of small communities in Jerusalem and Hebron there were no Jews living in the West Bank since that time. The land has been continuously populated predominantly by Arabs. Does this not count in your eyes?'

'It took the Jews three thousand years to return to their land. It's the only country we've got. And you want us to give it up?'

'You want the whole of the land to yourself and you're not even ready to share it. Don't you think this is discriminatory?'

'What's discriminatory about it? What's wrong with what we're doing? You want to walk? We have designated areas as natural parks which we forbid anyone, Arab or Jew, from building on. You and us can enjoy these areas.'

'I have not been able to enjoy these hills since your people came. I walk in fear of being shot at or arrested. There was a time when this place was like a paradise, a cultivated garden with a house by every spring. A small, unobtrusive house, built without concrete.'

'And then the Jews came like the serpent and ruined everything in the idyllic garden. You blame us for everything, don't you? But it doesn't matter. We've learnt our lesson from our long, tortured history. Here in our own land our existence is not premised on your acceptance. We've long since found out that we have to be strong if we are to survive here.'

There was little to say after this. But I made one last effort to alert him to what was being done to the land by those who claimed to love it. I said:

'The way it's going we'll end up with a land that is

criss-crossed with roads. I have a vision of all of us going around and around in circles. Whether we call it Israel or Palestine, this land will become one big concrete maze.'

He said nothing. He was still holding my wet hat. We were both standing up.

'Would you let me have my hat?' I asked. 'I want to continue with my walk.'

He stepped forward. I reached out and took the hat, turned my back and began walking. I could feel the settler's presence with his gun behind me. Then I heard him calling after me to stop. It felt more like an order which the law, his law, gave him the power to enforce. I feared for the worse.

'Would you like to smoke with me?' he asked.

I was taken aback by his offer. But I knew from experience that often the first impulse is the best one to follow and my intuition on this occasion was not to refuse.

I found myself a comfortable stone, and stretched my legs towards the water next to this settler on the bank of the little stream we each call by the same name, after the same tree, pronounced in our different ways, and accepted the *nergila* he passed to me.

As the strong stuff began to take effect, the memory of another *sarha* in these same hills came flooding back to me. That time I was with my friend Bishara in Wadi El Wrda at dusk. We sat on rocks by A'yn El Lwza below the cyclamen rock, not far from here. We had taken a long and satisfying walk and were resting before turning back. The sun was setting, the shadows cast by boulders were growing longer and denser. The colours were changing, transforming the hills we knew so well into a more muted world that we felt we had all to ourselves. Crossing our field of vision, like a phantom of the approaching doom, came a short man who was walking with long deliberate strides as though he was taking measurements. In the clarity of the moment I suspected the worst, tidings of a terrible future for our beautiful hills. A short time after this, work began on the settler road connecting Dolev to Beit Eil, which passed along the exact path this man had traversed. He must have been working for the Arab contractor who executed the work on behalf of the settlers. The hills were never the same after that.

We passed the mouthpiece between us and the smoke gurgled through the water. I inhaled and listened to the soft murmur of the stream as it slipped through the rocks and the birds singing and all the sounds and sights that I had blocked out. I began to feel guilty at what I was doing, willingly, sharing these hills with this settler. But then I thought: These are still my hills despite how things are turning out. But they also belong to whoever can appreciate them. If I postpone my enjoyment of them I might never achieve the *sarha* that I have sought for so long. As the Arab poet who was berated for drinking wine after the murder of his father said: *Al Yawm khamr wa ghadan imr* ('Today the wine; tomorrow is another day').

All the tension of the times, the worry about going through area C, the likely prospect of encountering soldiers or settlers, or getting shot at or lost was evaporating. With every new draw at the *nergila*, I was slipping back into myself, into a vision of the land before it became so tortured and distorted, every hill, watercourse and rock, and we the inhabitants along with it.

This young man was an artist at preparing a good *nergila*, I thought. He had talent.

'What's in this?' I asked.

'It's hashish that has been opiated.'

206

I was fully aware of the looming tragedy and war that lay ahead for both of us, Palestinian Arab and Israeli Jew. But for now, he and I could sit together for a respite, for a smoke, joined temporarily by our mutual love of the land. Shots could be heard in the distance, which made us both shiver. 'Yours or ours?' I asked. But how could we tell? We agreed to disregard them for now and for a while the only sound that we could hear was the comforting gurgle of the *nergila* and the soft murmur of the precious water trickling between the rocks.

ACKNOWLEDGEMENTS

The list of those who deserve recognition and thanks for the production of this book is long.

First my walking companions over the years: My wife Penny Johnson, my friends Bishara Dabit, Jonathan Kuttab, Henry Abramovitch, Jim and Debbie Fine, Saleh Abdul Jawwad, Rema Hamami, Alex Pollock, Elizabeth Taylor, Peter Coleridge, Rami Shehadeh, Mustafa Barghouti, Rami Abdulhadi, Iman Masri, Susan Rockwell, Emma Playfair and my niece and nephew Tala and Aziz. I thank all of them for being excellent walking companions.

Andrew Franklin, the Director of Profile Books, my publisher, friend and walking companion for his guidance, encouragement and editorial assistance. Colin Robinson, Senior Editor at Scribner, for his perceptive editorial assistance.

Kate Jones, the Director of ICM, my agent, for her editorial assistance, encouragement and support and her assistant at ICM Laura Sampson for her editorial support.

Penny Daniel, Nicola Taplin and Nassime Chida of

Profile Books for their much appreciated contribution to the production process of this book.

Kamal Abdul Fattah, the Palestinian geographer, for the wonderfully educational geographic trips throughout historic Palestine which he led in the 1980s before Israel imposed a complete ban on such trips and his help in identifying the names of the various locations mentioned in this book. Alex Baramki for his careful reading of various drafts, editorial suggestions and encouragement. Maya Yared for her careful reading and encouragement. David McDowall for his editorial assistance and helpful suggestions. Mark Handsley for his excellent copy editing of the manuscript. John Tordai, another walking companion, who contributed the evocative pictures that accompany the text.

And finally Penny, my partner throughout many of the difficult tribulations that I write about in this book, who has patiently endured my often insufferable moods during periods of distant reflection as I thought about the writing and then the mental turmoil that accompanies putting it all down on paper. Her sharp inquisitive and intellectually rigorous mind challenged me whenever I became uncritical, judgmental or slumped into intellectual indolence. Her editorial advice and assistance for the different drafts of this book were invaluable.

LIST OF ILLUSTRATIONS

211